HAUNTED
PETERBOROUGH

HAUNTED
PETERBOROUGH

Stuart Orme

The
History
Press

First published 2012

The History Press
The Mill, Brimscombe Port
Stroud, Gloucestershire, GL5 2QG
www.thehistorypress.co.uk

British Library Cataloguing in Publication Data.
A catalogue record for this book is available from the British Library.

ISBN 978 0 7524 7654 4
Typesetting and origination by The History Press
Printed in Great Britain

Contents

About the Author

STUART Orme was born and raised in Derby. He has a History degree from York University and an MA in Museum Studies, and has worked as a secondary teacher, adult education lecturer and freelance event organiser. Since 2001 he has worked for Peterborough Museum, where he is currently Interpretation Manager. He has a passion for history and is well known in the Peterborough area for delivering talks with enthusiasm and humour for local groups and societies. Stuart also leads guided tours of the city, including the Peterborough Ghost Walk (which he created), and regularly broadcasts on historical subjects on local radio.

The author in ghostly form in the museum's cellars. (Photograph by, and courtesy of, David Savory)

Foreword

OVER the past twenty-five years or so that I have been involved in the subject of ghosts, hauntings and the paranormal in general, I have been lucky enough to meet some very knowledgeable and scholarly people; my good friend Stuart Orme is one such person. His knowledge concerning the ghosts and hauntings of the city of Peterborough and its surrounding areas is second to none, and I for one am pleased that we now all have the chance to read about this city's ghostly side, thanks to this very book.

Stuart Orme takes us on a revealing journey, recounting a plethora of ghostly and paranormal encounters at such diverse places as the Peterborough Museum – a place I can personally vouch for as being haunted – and Peterborough's cathedral precincts, complete with ghostly monks, amongst other ethereal beings.

The variety of locations and stories that Stuart covers in *Haunted Peterborough* are pleasantly surprising; I was most interested to find chapters covering military ghosts ranging from Roman soldiers to Napoleonic prisoners-of-war and more, as well as hauntings associated with Peterborough's city centre buildings; how many of you have raised a glass or two within a haunted pub, or done your shopping at a place frequented by spectral inhabitants?

There is even a section containing information about the paranormal goings-on connected to everyday houses, as well as the far more grandiose stately homes which can be found in the region.

In his *Haunted Peterborough* publication, Stuart Orme has put together a fine collection which features accounts and stories of the strange and mysterious … and the thought-provoking.

Enjoy it. I certainly did!

Phil Whyman
Paranormal Investigator on TV's Most Haunted
Dead Haunted Nights Ghost Hunts

Introduction

'**S**URELY there aren't any ghosts in Peterborough? After all, it's only a new town …' This quote was from one incredulous visitor to Peterborough on being told that we ran a ghost walk in the city – and indeed, many people would be forgiven for thinking the same. The common perception by people who aren't well acquainted with the city is that it is somewhere they go through on a train, or that perhaps it is one of the artificial commuter towns north of London, like Welwyn Garden City or Milton Keynes. At best, people have heard of the cathedral.

This is unfair and inaccurate. Whilst Peterborough has greatly expanded since the Second World War and does have a high population of commuters, it also has a very

Postcard view of the cathedral and market place, c. 1920.

Church Street, c. 1900.

rich heritage. The area has produced some of the richest marine fossils in the world, many of which are now on display in the city's museum. At Flag Fen, on the eastern side of the city, the finest Bronze Age archaeological remains have been uncovered, and are preserved and displayed to visitors. The Romans built a fortress and town here – the centre of Roman Britain's pottery industry – and many examples of these pots are again displayed at the city's museum. It was only with the Anglo-Saxon occupation of the area that an abbey was founded, around which a market town sprang up. Today, these are Peterborough Cathedral and the city centre respectively. There is, of course, much more to the city and its surrounding villages than this, some of which will be revealed later in the book. For a more detailed look please visit the many fine attractions in the area, particularly the museum.

With this long history, it is perhaps not surprising that Peterborough should also have its own folklore, traditions and, above all, ghost stories. When initially conducting research for the Peterborough Ghost Walk in 2001, we uncovered some thirty different ghost stories within the area; that has now swelled as a result of ongoing research, people coming forward with their own stories, and, of course, a stream of new sightings, to number over 100 different ghostly happenings.

The ghost walk has proved to be so popular that it has attracted (at the time of writing) over 30,000 people onto it and is still going strong! This has been an excellent vehicle for entertaining and educating people about the rich history of this oft-overlooked city. If you happen to be in Peterborough and want to know more about some of these stories, you'd be advised to join one of the walks.

This book is also a way of publishing and highlighting many of the fascinating and unique ghostly experiences of the Peterborough area. Many of these tales have sadly, until now, been misreported or entirely neglected in print. This book represents just a sample of our local sightings; my choice of which to include has been capricious. I've picked out our most historic or public buildings, our best-documented hauntings, or simply those that provide the best stories. The accounts are not just concerned with the city centre, but with the suburbs, villages and countryside that make up the greater Peterborough area – the old 'Soke of Peterborough'. A substantial chapter has been dedicated to the museum alone, to try to record fully in print, for the first time, the range of paranormal activity that has been reported inside this remarkable building.

In writing this book I am indebted to all the people who have helped over the years in my researches – above all my colleagues and friends at Peterborough Museum over the last decade, who have supported my ghostly endeavours with interest, good humour and occasional long-suffering. I am grateful to Richard Hillier, Local Studies Librarian; Ben Robinson and Rebecca Casa-Hatton, past and present city archaeologists; and Gwen Beatty, Stephen Perry, Neil Mitchell and Steve Williams, all local historians, for providing the answers to some often very odd requests for information. I am also grateful to the *Peterborough Evening Telegraph* and BBC Radio Cambridgeshire for their help with public appeals for ghost stories, and for stimulating local interest over the years. Special mention goes to Brian Jones, fellow ghost-walk guide, for his input and additional stories; Nina Fereday for acting as chauffeur; and to Don Chiswell, Joe Chiswell and Chris Carr for proofing and commenting on the text.

I'd also like to say a big thank you to the numerous teams of ghost-hunters who have allowed me to tag along on their investigations over the years – including the Cambridge Paranormal Society, Dead Haunted, Fright Nights, the *Most Haunted* TV crew and too many others to list (sorry!) – on their visits to the museum. I'm particularly grateful to Phil Whyman for kindly agreeing to write the foreword. Above all, I'd like to thank all the people who have come forward and shared their ghostly experiences with me; it often requires more than a little courage to stand up and say 'this has happened to me'. Without them this book would not exist and it is therefore dedicated to those people.

Stuart Orme, 2012

Author's Note: Unless otherwise stated, all images are photographs taken by the author, or are original postcards or pictures from the author's collection. All other images are used with permission.

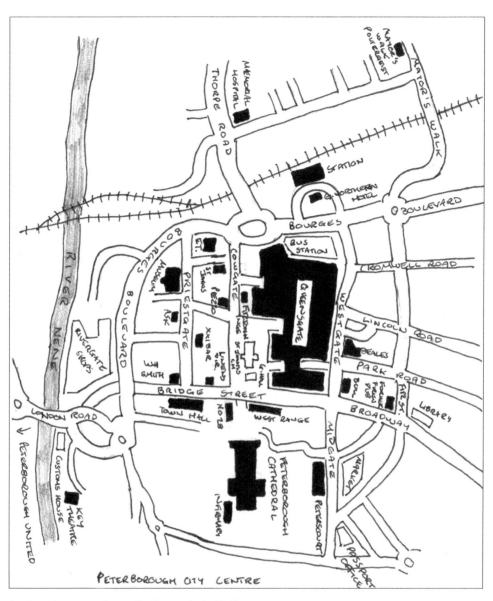

Peterborough city centre (haunted buildings marked in black).

Peterborough Museum

– Our Most Haunted Building

TUCKED at the end of Priestgate – a quiet street of Georgian buildings in the city centre, inhabited by firms of solicitors and accountants – is a grand stone building which houses the city's museum. Today the museum houses some 227,000 objects, covering all aspects of the city's history – from prehistoric marine reptiles to Britain's oldest murder victim; from manuscripts by the Romantic poet John Clare to craftwork by Napoleonic prisoners-of-war. Several of these collections are of national and international importance.

The building has a more sinister reputation; it is Peterborough's most haunted building and has at least eight different reported ghosts, with sightings or other phenomena reported regularly. As to why it is so haunted? Given the history of this remarkable building, it is perhaps not surprising …

The History of the Museum Building

The earliest known building on the site of the current museum dates back to the sixteenth century, when the property was acquired and a grand house built for the Orme family (whether or not they are ancestors to the author is unknown!). Humphrey Orme, Groom of the Bedchamber to Henry VIII, leased land in the manor of West Deeping in 1536 and sometime after this built a house, later known as Neville Place, in the nearby town of Peterborough in the affluent street of Priestgate. A grand house is marked on the spot in John Speed's map of 1611, and is shown clearly in the Prospect of Peterborough of 1731. The Orme family was one of the dominant families in the city; the empty tomb of

Peterborough Museum.

Sir Humphrey Orme can be seen today in the cathedral, vandalised by Cromwell's soldiers during the Civil War. His grandson, also called Humphrey, was MP for Peterborough during the 1650s and 1660s, and was responsible for the construction of the Guildhall on Cathedral Square; the Orme coat of arms can be seen displayed on the side of the building today.

In 1815 the Orme family had left and the property was initially leased, then sold, to one Thomas Cooke. Cooke, a businessman from Wortley in Manchester, had moved south and by 1815 was a city magistrate looking for a grand house to reflect his new status. The Orme house was substantially demolished and rebuilt in a grand Georgian style: this is the central part of the building which can be seen today. However, some of the original walls survived and were incorporated into the current building, most notably in the cellar. Features of the Georgian house also survive, including columns and a pediment over a doorway in the main reception area, and shuttered windows on the ground floor.

Upon Cooke's death in 1854 the building became vacant and was acquired by the second Earl Fitzwilliam on behalf of the Infirmary Trust, of which he was president. It was converted to become the Peterborough Infirmary, the city's first hospital, which was run on a charitable basis in the building until 1928. Various changes were made to the building during this period, particularly after a fire which severely damaged much of the upper floors in 1884. These alterations included a brick extension on the side of the building, with a kitchen, store-room and purpose-built operating theatre; a mortuary and bathhouse to the rear; and the wings, which can be seen today on either side of the main block (added in 1897 and 1902 respectively), to service the needs of the growing hospital.

Eventually the hospital, in this growing city, outgrew the Priestgate building. A new hospital was constructed on Thorpe Road, paid for by subscriptions as a memorial to the fallen of the First World War; this Memorial Hospital (until recently the Memorial Wing of the District Hospital) was opened in 1928. With patients transferred to the new facility, the Priestgate building again became vacant.

The building was bought by Percy Malcolm Stewart, Chairman of the London Brick Company, and donated to the Peterborough Museum Society as a permanent home for their collections. The society, originally called the Peterborough Natural History and Field Club, had been founded in 1871 by a group of like-minded individuals who were interested in local flora, fauna and history. Members included Dr Thomas Walker, surgeon at the Infirmary, and local chemist Mr Bodger. Collections of natural history, archaeology and general interest were acquired, and a permanent home sought. Previous venues for the museum included Becket's Chapel in the cathedral precincts and a house on Park Road.

The new museum was opened to the public in 1931, and originally occupied the ground floor and first floor of the building – the top floor being rented out to a local potato merchant, with the rent help-

The foundation stone laid by Thomas Cooke in 1816.

ing to pay for the running of the museum and the one paid member of staff, a care-taker. The museum continued to be run in this way until 1968, when the building and collections were given over to the care of Peterborough City Council. Since May 2010 the museum has been run by Vivacity, the Culture Trust for the city, and underwent a major refurbishment in 2011. Today the museum continues to fas-cinate and enthral visitors of all ages with a wide range of objects, from prehistoric monsters to the fine pieces of craftwork produced by Napoleonic prisoners-of-war at Norman Cross.

The Lonely ANZAC

The museum's most famous (or should that be infamous?) ghost is the figure of a man in grey, seen on the main staircase. This appa-rition is reputed to be the restless spirit of Australian soldier Sergeant Thomas Hunter, known to many as 'the lonely ANZAC'.

Thomas Hunter was actually born in England, in County Durham in 1880, but as a young man he emigrated to Australia, as many people did at that time. He eventually settled in the town of Kurri Kurri in New South Wales, where he worked as a coal miner. At the outbreak of the First World War in 1914 he enlisted with the Australian army and served with the 10th battalion of the 10th division, ANZAC (Australian and New Zealand Army Corps) forces. As part of this unit he fought at Gallipoli, then in the misery of the trenches of France and Belgium. It was here, during the Somme offensive of the summer of 1916, that Sergeant Hunter was seriously wounded. Taken to a field hospital, his condition was judged to be such that more advanced medical facilities would be needed in order to operate and remove the bullets lodged in his body. So, he was shipped back to England for surgery.

On arrival in Portsmouth, Hunter was placed on a hospital train bound for Halifax in Yorkshire, with other wounded men. As the journey went on his condition worsened, leading to the nurses on the train taking the unusual step of asking the driver if he would stop the train at the next avail-able station, so that Sergeant Hunter could be rushed to a nearby hospital for emer-gency treatment. The next such station happened to be Peterborough. The train was stopped and Hunter was rushed to the nearby Infirmary (today the museum), where sadly it was too late. He died in the building on 31 July 1916.

News of the story and death of Sergeant Hunter touched the hearts of Peterborians, who were perhaps moved by his plight because, in a sense, he represented all their own young men who were away fighting in the war. A public subscription fund was set up to pay for a memorial to Sergeant Hunter. A public funeral was held, in which the Mayor and civic dignitaries led the funeral cortège from the Infirmary to his final resting place at the Broadway Cemetery, during which virtually the entire city came to a stop and paid their respects. A 2m-tall granite cross was placed as a monument on Sergeant Hunter's grave, and a brass plaque to his memory mounted in the military chapel in the cathedral. Even today he is still commemorated in Peterborough, with an annual civic cer-emony held at his graveside on 25 April, international ANZAC Day. The ceremony is always attended by the Mayor, civic dignitaries and a representative from the Australian High Commission. It is said, though, that his spirit does not lie easily in that grave.

THE MUSEUM GHOST.

Noisy Visitors' Wait in Vain.

"GREY MAN" FAILS TO APPEAR.

The account of a spectral visitor to the upper purlieus of the Peterborough Museum, published last week, drew many people—curious, enquiring, and sceptical, to the old Town House of the Earls Fitzwilliam (and for many years the Infirmary), during the week-end. The story, as told by Mrs. Yarrow, the Caretaker's wife, and her daughter and which appears to be well founded, is that during the past year and more mysterious sounds as of someone walking have been heard at night in the Norman Cross room, once the Women's Surgical Ward. They have begun at eight and ceased with the closing of a door at about 2.30 a.m., and have been at their most intense at the waning of the moon. Mrs. and Miss Yarrow had become so accustomed to their ghostly visitor, who was in every way a well-behaved spectre, that they even named him Thomas, from the fact that he was first heard by them on St. Thomas' Day or Eve.

Account of Mrs Yarrow's sighting of the ghost, Peterborough Citizen, 3 May 1932.

There have been many sightings of a mysterious grey apparition around the building, most commonly gliding up the main staircase. It is said that this figure is the restless spirit of Sergeant Thomas Hunter.

The first documented sighting was in 1931, barely weeks after the museum was first opened to the public. At that time there was only one paid employee at the museum, by the name of Mr Yarrow, who acted as the caretaker. He lived on the premises, in a flat on the first floor, with his wife and two chil-dren. One afternoon he went out and left his wife alone in the building, to deal with the last few visitors and lock up at the end of the day. Mrs Yarrow duly locked up and returned to the flat in order to start preparing the evening meal, ready for when the family came home. After about half an hour she heard a noise echoing down the corridor from the main stairs and, assuming it was her husband returning home, went out to greet him. Coming out onto the corridor to collect some crockery from a cupboard, she observed through the glass panels in the doors leading out onto the main staircase that there was a figure coming up the stairs; not her husband but a man she said was about thirty years of age, dressed in a grey suit and with a slight 'phosphorescent glow'. To her astonishment, the figure vanished into thin air. Over the following months she saw him five times more; her daughter also witnessed him on a number of occasions.

These sightings were reported in the local newspaper, the *Peterborough Citizen*, in May 1932, and aroused a deal of local interest, prompting local children to regularly come into the museum at the end of the day in order to say goodnight to the ghost! According to the article, the ghost was known as Thomas because he was first seen on St Thomas' Day. The author has interviewed a former nurse from the days of the hospital, who maintained that the ghost had been seen before the hospital left the Priestgate building and that he had been positively identified as the spectre of Thomas Hunter. Interestingly, the ghost has always been seen in a grey suit – something which British and Australian wounded were issued with as a hospital uniform during the Great War.

Thomas Hunter's ghost has been seen on many occasions since then, usually at least once a year and most commonly around July and August, around the anniversary of his death. A few years ago he was seen by the young daughter of a member of staff in the museum staffroom, just off the main staircase. Having lunch with her father and mother in the room one Saturday, the little girl casually remarked to her astonished parents, 'Can I give a bit of my sandwich to the man in grey in the corner?' She then described the man; her account tallied exactly with that of the ghost, a description which she knew nothing about as her father had never told her, not wishing to frighten her or put her off coming into the museum.

In 2005 the ghost was seen twice, firstly by a Museum Officer locking up one evening. She locked up the top two floors, ensuring that there were no staff or visitors left there. As she headed back downstairs, she happened to glance back up and saw a grey figure standing at the top of the staircase. She went back to investigate but the figure was gone. A few months later, a young electrician working in the building was standing at the top of the main stairs one Thursday morning, waiting for his boss to come and give him instructions for the day. As he waited he stared out of the window, daydreaming, and glimpsed a grey figure walking past him out of the corner of his eye; when he turned to look, the figure was gone …

One of the most vivid sightings was a few months later, when another electrician also saw the ghost. Standing at the bottom of the stairs at about 6.30 p.m., waiting for a colleague who had gone to the toilet, he saw a grey figure appear halfway up the flight of stairs, glide up the staircase and then vanish. The rather shaken man later said that the figure didn't appear to walk up the stairs so much as 'glide up like a cloud of ash …'.

Prior to refurbishment, ghost-hunters occasionally observed the light fittings (which hung down the middle of the staircase on long cables) swinging for no apparent reason, like some form of strange pendulum. Was this the ghost of Thomas Hunter, or was it one of the museum's other spirits trying to draw attention to themselves? Many visitors and ghost-hunters have claimed to see or sense the restless spirit of Thomas Hunter. Most commonly, when people are in the Geology gallery on evening tours, guests or staff will catch a

Sergeant Thomas Hunter's grave, Broadway Cemetery.

17

glimpse of someone walking past the door; when they go to investigate, there is never anyone there … it seems he has no intention of leaving any time soon.

Death on the Stairs

Tucked away on the top floor of the museum building is an area not normally open to visitors. This part comprises a second staircase, a corridor, and rooms which are today used as office and storage space. Clues in the design of this area give an idea as to what it once was. The corridor is much narrower, the rooms smaller and the ceilings lower than the much airier ones throughout the rest of the building – denoting that some 150 years ago, in the days when this was a private house, this was the servants' quarters. The staircase would have been the servants' stairs, so they could get around the house whilst disturbing the family as little as possible.

We know from census records that the Cooke family kept five servants in 1851. The Orme house would also have had many servants to tend to the family. The wall on one side of the back staircase is some 3ft thick, much thicker than the rest of the Georgian building, indicating that it is possibly a remnant of the earlier house.

There is a piece of local folklore which I was told about shortly after starting work at the museum – that the ghost of a serving girl is said to haunt this staircase. According to the story this girl was a rather attractive young lady, which got her the unwelcome attentions of one of the male servants. When she refused his advances he forced himself on her and is said to have raped her on a number of occasions, as a result of which she became pregnant. She is then said to have stood at the top of these stairs one day and fallen – tumbling down to snap her neck and lie dead at the bottom. The reasons for her fall are unclear – did she fall, or maybe faint from morning sickness? Did she commit suicide, feeling sullied and desperate at her situation? Or did her tormentor push her down the stairs, wishing to dispose of her and the evidence of his crimes, her unborn child? There is no historical evidence to substantiate this story, not least as records from the earliest days of the private house are virtually non-existent.

Whatever the truth behind the tale, many people have reported strange phenomena in this area of the museum building, which have become associated with the ghost of this unhappy young girl. Interestingly, the overwhelming majority of phenomena reported in this area are witnessed by women. Sightings often include feelings of unease and even physical illness. The symptoms seem to be very similar to those experienced during morning sickness, even by women who have no knowledge of the legend associated with the stairs. A female voice and unaccountable noises have been heard in this area, audible to witnesses and picked up on recording devices. People have felt someone who they cannot see brushing past them on the stairs, and a dark figure has been observed sometimes halfway up the stairs.

Perhaps most disturbing of all, women who have been standing at the top of the staircase have complained about the sensation of having a pair of hands gently, but firmly, trying to push them down the stairs. Evidence perhaps that the girl was murdered? In 2005, during an organised ghost-hunt, one witness was deeply upset to see what she claimed was a 'grey disembodied hand' floating at the top of the stairs before vanishing up into the ceiling!

ridor was locked on what was a roasting hot day – the temperature on the corridor was probably in excess of 30 degrees. Then, almost at once, the hairs went up on the back of my neck and the temperature plunged … at which point I locked up and left that area very quickly!

Thomas and Charlotte Cooke

The current museum building was largely built in 1816 by Thomas Cooke, the local magistrate. Born in Manchester in 1777, the son of a wealthy industrialist, Cooke moved to London as a young man, where he met his first wife, Julia. Thereafter he moved to Peterborough, where the couple settled and had no less than twelve children, ten of whom survived into adulthood.

In 1817 Julia died. Two years later Cooke married again, this time to Charlotte Squire, daughter of a prominent local family. This family was already connected to Thomas Cooke by marriage – several years earlier, Charlotte's younger brother had married Thomas' oldest daughter by his first marriage; thus when Charlotte married Thomas she became her own brother's mother-in-law! In 1822 Thomas and Charlotte divorced, something which was regarded as being extremely scandalous in that period, as well as being legally difficult – an Act of Parliament was required in order to gain a divorce at that time. Charlotte moved into the Cookes' dower house next door, which survives today as a children's play centre. She died in 1850; Thomas died in his grand Priestgate house in December 1854.

Given the curious and often stormy relationship that the Cooke family had, as well as their links to the property, it is perhaps not surprising that their ghostly echoes have

The servants' stairs at the museum, haunted by a serving girl.

Being objective about these phenomena, the staircase is very old and atmospheric, and due to its age does lean very slightly. This could account for many reported experiences of feeling ill or disoriented, but it is remarkable how many reports of strange activity have come from this area and how they all seem to tally.

There have also been reports of cold spots and a male presence, as yet unidentified, along the old servants' quarters corridor. The author can attest to this from personal experience during his first month working at the museum in May 2001. Locking up alone one evening, I checked the cor-

been picked up around the building. Several mediums and psychics claim to have picked up the spirit of Thomas Cooke here, alleging to have identified a man by the name of Thomas who lived in the property, and who apparently still seems to regard the place with a proud and proprietorial air!

Charlotte's name has also been picked up on, most commonly associated with the main staircase. Female voices have been unaccountably heard in this area, some-thing which the author can attest to. On a number of occasions, when locking up after an evening tour around the museum, I have been so convinced that I have heard two women muttering together on the stairs that I thought I must have locked someone in the building by mistake. Upon investigation, there has never been anyone there …

During an organised ghost-hunt at the museum in 2003, a young couple were sat in the darkness at the top of the main staircase. At about 11.15 p.m. they heard a noise below, which they described as foot-steps going down the stairs, with a sound as if this person was wearing a long silk dress which was dragging on the steps. They then heard a female voice calling after this person: 'Lady Charlotte, Lady Charlotte!' They leaned over the stair rail to check but could see no one. They noted the time and thought nothing more of it. At the end of the evening, the ghost-hunters got together to compare notes and the couple related their experience. It transpired that two other ghost-hunters had been near the bottom of the staircase at the same time and had heard exactly the same sounds, completely independently. None of the ghost-hunters were aware of Charlotte Cooke's relationship to the property until I pointed it out to them. Does her unhappy ghost still visit the building?

Medical Ghosts – Dr Caleb Taylor and the Operating Theatre

Given that the museum building was the city's hospital for over seventy years, it is unsurprising that there should be some ghostly activity associated with this part of its history. Many people have reported unaccountably picking up on the 'smell'

The former dower house where Charlotte Cooke lived, later the Trinity Chapel.

of a hospital – disinfectants and so forth. Mediums have claimed to have seen the ghostly images of nurses, doctors and patients rushing around the building.

One of the foremost staff who worked at the Peterborough Infirmary when it was in the building was Alfred Caleb Taylor, the registrar. Taylor was a devoted medical practitioner and served the hospital well, gaining an enviable local reputation, second only to that of the surgeon Dr Thomas Walker. Taylor was also one of the first people in Britain (the first outside of London) to pioneer the use of the new X-ray photography in the early 1900s, even commandeering the porter's lodge as a dark room for developing his photographs, as it was the darkest place in the building. As the technology was very much in its infancy, the risks of the radiation used were not fully understood. Tragically, this cost Taylor his life; he died in 1927 of radiation poisoning.

The author has interviewed a lady who was brought up in the museum building in the late 1940s, when her father was employed as the museum caretaker. As such, they lived on the premises in the first-floor flat. One summer, the then little girl was laid low by a severe case of chickenpox and, as she lay in bed with the resulting fever, the doctor was sent for. The little girl woke up from her fever to see what she assumed to be the doctor sat at the bottom of her bed, a kindly-looking man in his late fifties with grey, balding hair, a moustache and round glasses. He smiled at her but said nothing, and after a few moments left the room. The little girl went back to sleep, awaking an hour later to find the actual doctor had come to visit. Who was it she had seen? The girl recovered quickly and some weeks later was helping her father tidy some photographs from the museum's collections.

The former operating theatre.

She was astonished to find a photograph of the man she had seen, which was identified as a picture of Alfred Caleb Taylor, a man who had died some twenty years earlier. Was his ghost still making house calls?

Off the main staircase of the building is a room which, until recently, had not been open to the public except for guided tours. It was being used as a laboratory for a team of volunteers who work on the many fine fossils discovered in the Peterborough area, and for which the museum is justly famed. A member of the *Most Haunted* film crew, when entering this room during the team's visit in April 2005, claimed to have felt someone walk through them, and got a cold sensation on their hand, which they described as being as if a small child was invisibly trying to hold their hand for reassurance. Why should there be such phenomena in this room? This was the hospital's operating theatre, and is still complete with its original tiled walls and floors, large windows and a skylight to admit as much light as possible to illuminate the surgeon's work. We know that there were operations which were not successful, where people died on the operating table. As part of the museum's refurbishment, the room has now been restored. Will these spirits return to visit, among the newly reinstated surgical equipment?

The Girl in the Gallery

One of the museum's most prized collections is its extensive and rich array of fossils, all found locally. The geological conditions around Peterborough are excellent for preserving these creatures from the past, and the marine dinosaurs on display at the museum are some of the best in the world. The gallery in which they are displayed on the first floor of the museum also has a more supernatural resident, with many people picking up on the spirit of a little girl. Who this little girl is or was is unknown. It is unclear what stage of the building's history she comes from (if any); various mediums and psychics have come up with their own explanations, none of which seem to tally thus far with any historical evidence. Many people come up with the name Amy or Anna for her.

There is a traditional Victorian saying, that 'Children should be seen and not heard'. This particular ghost seems to subscribe to the opposite point of view. She is seen very rarely. In 2004 she was seen by a young workman working in a corridor (formerly part of the caretaker's flat) just off

the Geology gallery. Working up a ladder on some wiring down the corridor, the workman heard a noise behind him. At the end of the corridor is a closed door with two frosted glass windows in it, through which he saw the figure of a little girl going past on the other side. Knowing that there was a school party visiting that morning, the young man assumed that this girl was lost and went to see if she was alright. As he pushed the door open he was horrified to see that there was nobody there; not only that, but all that was there on the other side of the door was a cupboard – no way any child from a school party could have been in there in the first place!

The doorway where the apparition of the little girl was seen in 2004.

The most recent sighting of her (at the time of writing) was in December 2008, when she was seen by a member of the public on a commercial ghost-hunt. This particular gentleman had come along as an avowed sceptic, to keep his girlfriend company. At one point during the evening, he was alone near the period shop display when he was astonished and terrified to see the figure of a little girl appear and disappear in the glass of the window. The description he gave of her tallied exactly with those of previous sightings, even though no such description has ever been published. The gentleman left the building that night very unnerved and rather less of a sceptic.

The ghost of the little girl has been heard more often. In 2003, the author was spending the evening in the museum with a group from the Cambridge Paranormal Society. I was in the Geology gallery at around midnight with two members, Paul and Angela, doing a test known to ghost-hunters as an EVP (Electronic Voice Phenomena) test. This involved placing a tape recorder on a table in front of us, and asking questions of any spirits in the vicinity, hoping to prompt a response on the recording which could not have been heard by the human ear alone. The inevitable first question is: 'Is there anybody there?' then the remaining questions went on for about ten minutes. When the recording was replayed after the first question, the sound of a small girl answering 'Yes' was heard … although no response was picked up to any of the other questions.

Another recording was taken in January 2008 by a group of local ghost-hunters. A digital recorder had been left in the Geology gallery for a period of about three hours, and the room locked off so that there could be no human intervention.

Upon playing the recording back at leisure some days later, the ghost-hunters heard nothing but silence for the first hour, then a loud inexplicable BANG. There was then further silence for an hour, before the sound of a little girl's voice saying, 'Mum.' Recordings of the girl laughing were taken in June 2010.

Similar experiences and recordings have been noted by other investigators; it seems that although this little girl may keep her identity to herself, she is keen to communicate with the living, given the right opportunity …

A Roman Visitation

One of the many fine objects on display in the museum's Archaeology gallery on the first floor of the building is an original Roman sword. This prized exhibit was discovered in 1975 in the area of the former large inland lake known as Whittlesey Mere. Dating from the first century AD, this rusted piece of iron is a rare surviving example of a Roman cavalry sword, a replica of which can be seen displayed nearby. Over the years, several people have reported 'odd' happenings in relation to this particular object, especially if it has been moved. Individuals have had a suspicion that they are being watched, as if the original owner was keeping a careful eye on it!

Investigators from the Cambridge Paranormal Society conducted a trial in 2004, when they brought a female psychic into the museum under controlled conditions. The lady was not allowed to look around the building initially, but asked to sit in a room downstairs and try to contact any spirits within the museum. She claimed to have made contact with the ghost of a Roman soldier from the 9th Legion, who had been stationed in the area; significantly, she identified that he was from Spain, that he rode a horse, and that he was connected to an object in the building. A member of the group was asked to go out of sight of the medium and walk around a Roman exhibition downstairs, whilst the lady would call out when the spirit told her that the person was next to their 'lost property'. The object that the investigator was asked to stop by was the sword.

As previously mentioned this is a cavalry sword, unusual for the Roman army which was overwhelmingly composed of infantry. And interestingly, the 9th Legion was nicknamed the 'Hispania' by the Romans as the men were predominantly recruited from Spain.

In September 2006, a group was spending the night in the museum as part of a commercial ghost-hunt. At around 11.30 p.m. everyone had gone downstairs for a coffee break, apart from two men who remained at the top of the main museum stairs to take photographs. From their vantage point, they saw a dark figure cross the first-floor corridor from the Geology gallery into the Archaeology gallery. They shot down the stairs to investigate; as they got to the door of the room, they saw a dark, male figure standing at the end of the gallery, looking into the case containing the Roman sword. The figure turned and then disappeared behind a nearby display. One of the men stood in the doorway to stop the figure from leaving; the other went in and searched the room … and found no one. The only other way out of that room was an alarmed fire door, which wasn't triggered. So who, or what, was it they saw?

A group spending the night in the building in January 2007 observed a square, wooden building block roll 3ft out from under a table in the room, with no apparent reason and nobody physically anywhere near it. Was the Roman trying to attract their attention, or does the room have more than one spirit visitation?

The White Lady

On the top floor of the museum is the Changing Lives gallery, which records the more recent history of the city through the nineteenth and twentieth centuries: how people have lived, worked and died in the city. This room has also been connected with a number of paranormal phenomena reports, the most common of which is the

The Archaeology gallery; a ghostly figure was seen here by two men in 2006.

Foundation stone for the 1902 Infirmary extension.

unaccountable smell of burning. Visitors, staff and ghost-hunters have picked up on a strange burnt smell in this gallery, which can appear and disappear within moments, with no apparent explanation. One more unusual explanation for this smell is that, in 1884, a significant fire broke out in this part of the building, which led to the then hospital being evacuated. The fire gutted the top floor and made the building unusable for some six months whilst repairs were carried out. Is the smell some form of psychic leftover from the event, or is there a more rational explanation yet to be found?

Visitors to the museum have also seen that most traditional of apparitions, a White Lady, in this room. She has been most commonly seen on quiet afternoons by members of the public visiting the museum; who she is and why she haunts the building is unknown. A gentleman from out of town, visiting the museum one wet Wednesday afternoon in 2003, came downstairs to ask surprised staff if the building was haunted, and then proceeded to tell them that he had been followed round the gallery by 'a white figure'. As he rounded each corner of the gallery, he would catch a glimpse of this white female figure behind him out of the corner of his eye; when he looked back properly the figure was gone, but as he rounded the next corner the same thing would happen.

In November 2007, two ladies visiting the museum were astonished to get a good look at the White Lady. Up in the gallery, looking in cases on either side of an aisle, they felt the hairs go up on the back of their necks and saw a white figure materialise behind them, glide between them and just vanish. The two ladies concerned were understandably shaken as a result. Incidentally, the most recent sighting, in October 2008, was also by two women during the daytime.

The author has mixed feelings on the subject of mediums and psychics; whilst I have seen many genuine people trawl the museum and come up with some interesting information, I have seen many more who are sadly obvious frauds. The most convincing demonstration of mediumship I have seen thus far was by a spiritualist medium called Bill, brought in under controlled conditions (i.e. having not been told where he was going, so he could not conduct research in advance) by members of the Cambridge Paranormal Society. He went around the building picking up a few details, but nothing very profound until he came into the Changing Lives gallery. Here he suddenly announced the presence of an eight-year-old boy, who had died after an unsuccessful operation performed on his stomach in the building in 1908. He gave dates, a name, even the street in Peterborough on which the boy had lived. I later looked in the house surgeons' records in the museum collection to verify this information. These are the original hand-written books; there are no copies, they are not on display, they have never been published, and they are not available on the Internet – in other words, I can be satisfied that he cannot have had sight of them. When I found the date in question in the book, there was the little boy, with every detail the medium had told us being correct. One has to ask, how on earth could he have known?

The Dark Man

On the first floor of the museum, a popular area for people to visit is the period shop: a recreation of a general store which stood in Peterborough in the early 1900s. Many visitors spend a lot of time peering through the shop windows, trying to identify the goods that would have been on sale in that period and comparing them to products available today.

Some visitors, however, feel very uncomfortable in this area. To some extent this could be because it is the darkest part of the building, with no natural light and limited artificial lighting, which can create a psychosomatic response; whatever the reason, people have had very adverse reactions here. Some visitors just walk into this area, shudder and walk out for no apparent reason.

A small boy, who is a regular visitor to the museum with his mum, came to the period shop one afternoon in 2004. Normally, the two of them would spend time looking in the shop window, seeing how many groceries they could recognise from the supermarket today. On this occasion, the little boy came in first and started screaming; his mum rushed to investigate but found nobody there apart from her son. Staff investigated, security cameras were checked … but there was no sign of anyone. All the little boy would say was that there was a 'nasty man there'.

This dark figure has been seen lurking in this area by both visitors and ghost-hunters. Who this man is and why he haunts the area is unknown, although a clue was given by the *Most Haunted* TV crew during their visit in 2005. Spiritualist medium David Wells picked up on the spirit of an individual called George Wilson, who he said was a First World War soldier, treated in the building for severe burns received during

Peterborough Infirmary, c. 1910.

fighting in France. No evidence has been found thus far to substantiate a connection between this man and the Infirmary.

Strange light anomalies have been seen in this area, and a floating series of lights or 'orbs' were picked up on video by the Cambridge Paranormal Society. Footsteps have been heard by people conducting vigils here; some have even claimed that they were poked or prodded by an unseen person. Whether this is really the spirit of George Wilson, or perhaps that of one of the other ghosts connected to the building, remains to be seen.

Norman Cross Gallery

The Norman Cross gallery on the top floor of the building houses one of the museum's most prized collections – an assortment of French prisoner-of-war work, probably the finest of its kind in the world. These items were made at the world's first purpose-built prisoner-of-war camp, built to the south of Peterborough, near Yaxley, in 1797 to house Napoleonic prisoners (for more details on the story of the camp – and indeed the ghostly happenings there since – *see* Chapter Three).

Until 2005, no supernatural phenomena had ever been reported inside this room; indeed, many ghost-hunters had described it as the perfect room to have a rest in! Then, after some refurbishment work in the gallery, things started to happen. This is not uncommon; many old buildings report no paranormal phenomena for years, until building works or alterations take place – almost as if the change stirs things up.

Various ghost-hunters have reported catching a glimpse of a figure in the corridor outside the gallery, walking past the door. Who, or what, this person is isn't known. Others have reported seeing a ghostly animal in the gallery. Witnesses have variously described this as being a large cat or a small dog, the uncertainty due to the fact that this spectral creature is rather misty and indistinct, but definitely small and four-legged!

In November 2006, Phil Whyman, former paranormal investigator of Living TV's *Most Haunted*, was taking part in a vigil in this gallery as part of a commercial ghost-hunting event run by his company, Dead Haunted. Phil is a very grounded individual, who says that in nearly twenty years of ghost-hunting he has rarely seen something he cannot explain. On this occasion, he was sat in a corner of the Norman Cross gallery with a guest. The lights were out, but, due to the ambient lighting from emergency lights and their eyes having adjusted from being in the room for about half an hour, they could see reasonably well. As they were talking, Phil became aware of something reaching over his shoulder, and was astonished to see a bare male hand and arm, rather dirty and hairy, reach over towards his face. He moved away quite quickly and turned to look behind … only to see that the arm had gone.

This room bore witness to one of the rare occasions when paranormal phenomena was caught on CCTV camera at the museum. In June 2007, a ghost-hunting group from Derby was spending the night in the building. They conducted a vigil for about half an hour in this room, then retired to the ground floor for a restorative cup of coffee before continuing. They returned about half an hour later and were astonished to find a plastic mast from a model boat in the middle of the floor. They swore that it had not been there when they had left the room. We checked the CCTV footage and found that the area where the mast was found was covered by an automatic security light, which is triggered by a motion sensor. We watched the recording and, sure enough, when the investigators left the room the light was triggered. The recording showed them leaving the room and revealed that the floor was clear. The automatic light remained on for about forty-five seconds after they had left, then went out. All we could see next was darkness. About thirty minutes later, the light went back on as the investigators came back in and, even before any of them could reach the section of the room where the mast had appeared, it was there – shown on the camera – in the middle of the floor. Human intervention could be ruled out, as it would be impossible for anyone to put the mast on the floor without triggering the automatic light and thus showing up on the recording. So, how did it get there?

The Caretaker

One of the most commonly used rooms in the museum is the Martin Howe lecture room on the ground floor. This multi-functional space is used for school parties for some of the many vibrant education sessions offered at the museum; evening room hire for community groups; events at weekends; and even as a base room for would-be ghost-hunters investigating the building.

Like most of the building, this room has a curious history. During the days of the hospital, this was the out-patients' waiting room and was initially used for surgical procedures before a proper operating theatre was added in 1897. Quite what those waiting to see the doctor made of the dubious experience of hearing an operation being carried out on the other side of a curtain can only be imagined. It is possible that it did wonders for any hospital waiting lists!

Various mediums and psychics have claimed that this room is visited by the spirit of a caretaker. Some even claim to have seen him: a stooping man in his fifties, who skulks round the edge of the room with a large bunch of keys at his belt. It is unknown who this man is, what period of the building's history he comes from, or why he haunts the place.

The caretaker may be the reason why furniture has, on occasion, been mysteriously moved around overnight. One of the most dramatic examples of this was in 2001, when a Museum Officer set out the room ready for a school party the following day, using brightly coloured plastic chairs and low tables. On a whim, he decided to use red chairs on one side of a table and blue on the other. Being the last to leave, he then locked up the building and went home. This man was then the first into the building the following morning and was astonished to find that the chairs had been moved. They were now arranged alternately red then blue around the table. Checking the alarm logs he found that nobody had been into the building overnight, so who – or what – had moved the chairs? Perhaps the caretaker is still looking for gainful employment …

Banging and Shoving

The ground-floor galleries of the museum are perhaps the least active parts of the building, but even they have had strange phenomena reported. Visitors in the second, rearmost exhibition gallery have commented on having the strong sensation that, if they are near the end of this room, they are being watched, or even that an unseen individual is standing right behind them. In 1998, a girl on work experience at the museum was assisting with producing labels for an exhibition in this gallery – on a Monday, when the building was closed to the public. Alone and at the back of the room, she suddenly found herself pushed violently to the floor. She turned round quickly, to find absolutely nobody there.

The front exhibition gallery has also had occasional ghostly activity. Several visitors have felt uncomfortable near the entrance to the toilets, and on two occasions an apparition of a cowled figure, described as being 'like a monk', has been seen there. Over the years, some staff working in the evening in one of the galleries have caught glimpses of someone walking past the door in the main corridor outside. When they go to investigate, there is no sign of anyone.

The author can also attest to some of the paranormal activity in this area. In January 2004, I was alone in the building one Monday evening at about 6.30 p.m. All the other staff had already left and I was about to go home for the day. Having just locked my office upstairs, I headed downstairs, and then suddenly remembered that I needed to send an urgent e-mail before leaving. Rather than go back upstairs, I sat and used the computer terminal at the front reception desk, opposite the closed and locked double doors leading to the front exhibition gallery. I sat typing for a few moments, when there were suddenly three enormous bangs on the other side of the gallery doors, as if someone was hammering on them with a fist. Astonished, I hurried over to the doors and unlocked them, only to find … absolutely nothing. Nobody there; no apparent explanation for the noises. I spent twenty minutes afterwards trying to replicate the noise; the only way that I could do so was by hammering with a fist (so it was really painful!) as hard as possible. To this day, I have still not managed to find a rational explanation for what caused that noise. It was only when I got home that I started shaking.

The front gallery doors, where the author heard knocking.

'There was something down there with me' – the Museum's Cellar

Of all the areas in the museum, the one that has perhaps the most sinister reputation is the old cellar underneath the core of the building. This area is not generally open to the public, but guided tours are often taken down there – partly because they are a fascinating insight into the story of the building, and partly due to their ghostly reputation. This was made famous by the *Most Haunted*

team on their visit to the museum, when one of the doors in the cellar slammed on the crew, allegedly by its own devices.

These cellars are as old as the site itself; much of the stonework and even a window frame can be seen from the original Tudor house. The remainder of the stonework dates to Thomas Cooke's Georgian mansion, and retains the original fittings for wine and coal cellars in two of the subterranean rooms. The underground rooms would have provided cold storage for many items in the days when the building above was a private house; and it has been suggested that, in the early days of the Infirmary, the rooms were used in the summer for the storage of cadavers (a former stable building at the back was used in the winter), until a proper mortuary was constructed to the rear. During the Second World War, the resident caretaker and his family used the cellar as an air-raid shelter during the bombing of the city centre. One of the cellar rooms still retains traces of its use as the shelter. In more recent times, it has been used for general storage of scenery for museum exhibitions.

Compared to many of the museum's phantoms, recorded sightings have been relatively recent. The first sign that something was odd took place in the mid-1980s, when workmen installing the new security and alarm system were working in this area. They became very uncomfortable about working in the cellar on their own – not least when they started hearing voices or footsteps when they were down there alone.

In 2001, a man from the electricity board went into the cellar to read the meter. Collecting the key to the cellar from reception, he went down on his own – then came back a few moments later as white as a sheet. All he would say was that, whilst

The museum cellar corridor.

he had been down in the cellar, 'There was something down there with me.'

Since then the cellar has been opened up to tours and ghost-hunters, and reports have increased dramatically. Various phenomena have been reported, including the experience of a group of young ladies on a ghost-hunt in 2006, who were terrified when they claimed to see a phantom, misty dog creeping down the cellar corridor.

A commonly seen apparition is that of a hooded monk or priest – perhaps associated with the original Tudor house, as some members of the Orme family seem to have retained the Catholic faith after the Reformation. The figure has been seen a couple of times a year on average, on one occasion by four people all at the same time, one of whom was the author. There were four of us sat in one of the rooms in the cellar, waiting to see if anything would happen. After about twenty minutes of sitting in the semi-darkness, a figure started to slowly appear in the doorway, that of a hooded monk. It was there for a few seconds then slowly faded away again. All four of us saw the figure; its slow materialisation was rather like watching the contrast being changed on a television set.

The other spook in the cellar can be less than hospitable. When seen he appears to be a small, hairy individual in dirty clothes, rather reminiscent of Baldrick, the scruffy servant to Blackadder in the television comedy. He is perhaps the spirit of a servant from the days of the house, who knew the cellars well and still regards them as his space. As such, he will sometimes try to scare people out. Moans, groans and footsteps have been heard in the cellar, and small stones or nuts (minus the bolts) have gone flying off a shelf past people. On one occasion, in 2005, a young lady in the cellar was standing in darkness in an end room during an organised ghost-hunt. She said that she felt a dark figure suddenly appear behind her right shoulder, lean over her shoulder and moan into her ear. She screamed and fled the cellar at this point – climbing over your correspondent, who was coming through the doorway to investigate the scream, in her haste to get out.

A Haunted Car Park?

The car park behind the museum has also been the site of paranormal activity. This was originally where the gardens were behind Cooke's house, and was later the site of various ancillary buildings for the hospital. These included a bathhouse, which was open to the public (the slipper baths) and was later set aside for decontamination

The Trinity Street car park. The brick building is part of the mortuary; the painted sign relates to the wartime decontamination centre.

purposes in the event of a gas attack during the Second World War.

It was also the site of the hospital's mortuary – a building that was later used as the local Scout headquarters – and, perhaps because of its previous use, gained a reputation for being haunted. Former Scouts and Scout-leaders complained of a cold presence in the building, and told me that if they ever stayed there overnight, they would never get a restful night's sleep.

Since this building was demolished, the area has been used as a car park for local businesses during the day, and for the public at night and weekends. People coming back to their cars late at night have complained of being touched or clapped on the shoulder by an invisible cold hand. In addition, a white figure has been seen walking across the car park. Are these spirit visitors anything to do with the fact that the hospital's dead were stored on this site in times past?

2

Monks and More ...

Ghosts of the Cathedral

THE very heart of the city of Peterborough, physically, historically and spiritually, is the cathedral. Without this magnificent building, Peterborough would simply not exist; although, with its long story, there have inevitably been darker chapters. As a result of these events, it is perhaps understandable that a number of ghosts are said to haunt the area around the cathedral. Indeed, if the museum is the most haunted building in the city, the precincts would seem to be the most haunted area. If you walk through the cathedral's environs, you never know what you might see ...

History of the Cathedral

There has been a church on the cathedral site since Peada, the Anglo-Saxon prince (and briefly king) of Mercia, founded an abbey in AD 655. This became one of a number of monasteries in this area: the 'fen five' of Thorney, Ramsey, Crowland, Ely and the abbey of St Peter at what is now Peterborough. The monastery, and the town that grew up around it, were twice the scene of violence from Viking invaders.

In AD 870, the wooden abbey was attacked and destroyed by Vikings – perhaps a part of the 'great heathen army' that invaded East Anglia that year. A piece of Anglo-Saxon carving that is alleged to have come from the original abbey can be seen displayed inside the cathedral today, the famed 'Hedda stone'. The abbey was rebuilt a century later by Bishop Aethelwold of Kent, only to be attacked again in 1070 when it was sacked by an army of Danish mercenaries led by Hereward. He claimed that he was stopping the wealth of Peterborough from falling into the hands of the Normans, but still torched the whole town apart from the abbey church itself. With a bizarre Peterborough logic, a radio station and shopping centre have, in more recent times, been named after Hereward, despite the fact that he caused such devastation here!

The ongoing story of the abbey was by no means peaceful. In 1103 the abbey was looted by Flemish mercenaries. Barely a generation after the firestorm of Hereward, the entire abbey, church and town were destroyed in the 'great fire' of Peterborough in 1116. Like the Great Fire of London 550 years later, the fire was said to have started in a baker's shop. The chronicler Hugh

Above: *Peterborough Cathedral.*

Right: *The Norman gateway into the precincts, c. 1900.*

Candidus blamed this on Abbot John de Seez losing patience with his monks and telling them to 'go to the Devil', followed by the monk's baker invoking the Devil to try and light the fire in his ovens. The Devil was said to have taken the invitation and burnt the abbey down!

Undaunted, the Benedictine monks – famed for their black robes, financial acumen and work ethic – began to build again, commencing work in 1118 on their new monastic church. The building which they completed some 130 years later is the one that we see today. During the Middle Ages both town and abbey became prosperous, earning the nickname 'gilden-burgh', the golden borough. It was a minor centre of pilgrimage, with holy relics of St Oswald and St Thomas Becket. The area was also attacked during the Peasants' Revolt of 1381, by locals who were incensed over increased taxation (leading to a bloodbath in the town square), and by soldiers looting and pillaging in 1461 during the Wars of the Roses.

The abbey church was closed in 1539 when Henry VIII dissolved the monastery; in 1541 it was established as the cathedral church for the new Diocese of Peterborough. Two queens have been buried there; Katharine of Aragon, the first of Henry VIII's six wives, in 1536, and Mary Queen of Scots in 1587. Mary was hastily buried in Peterborough after her execution at Fotheringhay Castle, only to be moved to Westminster Abbey in London two decades later. The cathedral was sacked by Cromwell's soldiers during the Civil War, with major damage being caused. Thankfully, less damage was caused by the German bombs which fell on the church during the Second World War. Today the cathedral precincts are an oasis of calm in the midst of a busy city centre, and an essential stop for visitors to the city.

The West Front Stonemason

The most photographed view in Peterborough – indeed, one of the top ten views in Britain, so a recent poll has revealed – is the marvellous West Front of Peterborough Cathedral. This magnificent example of Early English Gothic style is an architectural marvel, with its three enormous arched gables looming over the green at the heart of the precincts. Above each arch are four slit windows. One of the windows above the left-hand arch is, so legend has it, haunted by the ghost of one of the men who built this magnificent church.

The story has it that the man had worked on the church all his life – since childhood, when he had been apprenticed to be a stonemason. He was now aged about fifty, a good age in a time when people were not as long-lived as today. He was desperate to see the church completed before he died, and thus see his life's work complete. Accordingly, he would often stay late into the night, even after everyone else had gone home, to do extra work and try to speed the building work along.

One night he was working late by the light of a candle, perched high up on wooden scaffolding inside the building. Eventually, in the early hours of the morning, he tired and so packed up his tools to go home, lowering his tool bag down from the scaffolding on a rope. He then double-checked with his lamp to make sure he had not left anything; then, as he turned to leave, his candle blew out. Unable to locate his flint and steel to relight his candle, he tried to navigate his way in the dark – only to lose his footing and plunge from the scaffolding to his death.

A candle has been seen glowing in one of these upper windows late at night by those passing through the precincts, even though there should be no person, let alone a burning candle, inside. Legend has it that this is the light of the ghostly stonemason

The West Front, c. 1880; the stonemason haunts a window above the left-hand arch.

35

– the candle that cost him his life – whilst the spirit of the stonemason himself is said to come back to the inside of the window, still chipping away at the window frame he never got to finish.

Benedictine Monks

The most common ghosts experienced around the cathedral precincts are ethereal monks. Given that the site was a monastery for some 900 years, this is perhaps hardly surprising. Many people claim to have encountered the ghostly figures of black-clad, hooded Benedictine monks.

The Monk in the Cloisters

A ghostly monk has been seen once or twice a year walking across the ruined cloisters on the side of the cathedral. People who have seen him say he appears so clearly that they often mistake him for a real person. An American lady, a tourist visiting Peterborough, was in the cloister in 1996, taking some pictures at twilight on a summer's evening. As she was looking through the viewfinder on her camera, she caught a glimpse of the hooded figure of a monk emerging from a doorway in the corner of the cloister; he then walked diagonally across the cloister towards the cathedral. Assuming it was someone dressed up for a performance, or perhaps even a member of the clergy, the lady ignored the figure and carried on taking her pictures. The figure then disappeared into a doorway in the shadows. Once she had finished her photography, the woman decided she would follow the figure; if there was a performance or service going on then she would like to take part. However, when she went

to investigate, she was horrified to find that the hooded figure had appeared from a doorway that was blocked up with stonework, and had disappeared into a locked door on the side of the cathedral.

In 2001, a local lady was walking her dog through the precincts on the eve of a large medieval re-enactment event (the precursor of the current annual Peterborough Heritage Festival). She went past the period market and living history displays as they were setting up around the precincts, and walked down the alleyway to the right of the West Front, leading through to the ruins of the cloister. As she walked into the alleyway, a figure dressed as a monk came through the archway at the other end. He appeared to be a solid figure, but she

The passage leading to the cloister; a phantom monk has been seen here.

could not see his face as his hood was up and pulled low. As there were many other people in period costume around the precincts that evening, the lady thought little of this and carried on walking down the alleyway; she only said later that, as the figure walked past her, she became aware of the air turning slightly cold. After a few minutes in the cloister the lady came back out, and got chatting to a couple of the re-enactors on the cathedral green. During the conversation, she was rather unnerved to find that not only had they not seen anyone emerge from the alleyway – despite the fact that they had been in clear view of it all the time – but that there was nobody present over the weekend dressed as a monk. Interestingly, during the setup for the summer 2011 Heritage Festival, another local woman had a similar experience. Perhaps the presence of large numbers of costumed characters around the precincts encourages this particular monk to put in an appearance.

Monks inside the Cathedral

Another ghostly monk has been seen inside the cathedral. He has his hood pulled back, unusually, so his face can be seen. He appears to be a young man of about eighteen years, dressed in a monk's black habit, who looks very tired and hungry. On each occasion he has been seen he has done exactly the same thing. He is said to walk up the cathedral nave, then stop suddenly and look behind him. When he turns back he looks petrified and then appears to be running in terror from someone, only to vanish near the front of the nave under the great tower. One account I have of a sighting of this ghost goes back to the 1960s, when a lady from Spalding brought her mother to visit the cathedral. Although the lady herself saw nothing, as soon as they walked into the cathedral, her mother went very quiet and kept glancing over her shoulder. It was only when they left the church a short while later that the mother told her daughter what she had seen. The lady told me that her mother was very level-headed and steadfastly refused to believe in ghosts, but firmly believed in what she saw that day.

A curious observation from witnesses is that this ghost's feet cannot be seen, almost as if he is running on a level below the current floor surface. This might fit the pattern of 'stone tape' hauntings, which are common in many sites (for discussion of this theory, *see* Afterword). One suggestion is that this ghost is that of a monk from one of the earlier monastic churches, buried beneath the current building. Could he be running in terror from Viking raiders, his feet not visible to us as the floor he knew is below the current one? Does he vanish at the spot where the Vikings caught up with him? If so, it does not take much imagination to guess what happened to him next.

A choir is occasionally heard inside the cathedral. Nothing unusual in that, as the cathedral does have its own excellent choir. The problem is that, on some occasions, the choir appears to be non-existent other than the sound. Witnesses report invisible male voices singing in Latin, when no recording is playing – perhaps ghostly monks saying their prayers from beyond the grave. Polly Howat, in her book *Ghosts and Legends of Cambridgeshire*, records how local historian Trevor Bevis went into the cathedral during a lunch break from work in November 1958. Virtually alone in the building, he heard a choir singing with great sweetness and spiritual power, despite the fact that no choir was there. The Latin chant swelled to the point that he believed he could reach out and touch the invisible monks around him. After a few moments, the singing stopped and Trevor left. On the way out he met and talked to one of the vergers, who confirmed that he was not the first to have heard the choir. The author has met two other people who have had a similar experience over the last decade.

Ghosts in the Graveyard

To the north side of the cathedral (the left side as one looks at the West Front) is the ancient graveyard. Few burials other than those of senior clergy have taken place here in recent centuries, but once it was the main burial ground in Peterborough. It was originally much larger, but it was reduced when part of its land was swallowed up by the private deer park established by Abbot Robert Kirkton for his private amusement around 1500. Space was at such a premium by the Tudor period that our famed

gravedigger from this time, 'Old Scarlett' (Robert Scarlett, who lived to be ninety-eight), would often dig up old bones to make way for new burials. Even so, bodies were buried in multiple layers, and the effect of this is evident at the edge of the cathedral – the sharp drop from the edge of the graveyard to the church foundations and natural ground level is caused by the congestion of corpses. The graveyard only ceased to be the main town burial place in 1803, with the opening of the new parish burial ground at the end of Cowgate. By now, the cathedral graveyard had become a public health hazard, with subsidence caused by rotting bodies proving to be a danger to those passing through.

In this area and beyond, a number of ghostly figures have been seen. Two phantom monks have been observed in the gateway alongside the West Front of the cathedral, which leads into the graveyard; one standing, the other kneeling as if praying. Another ghostly monk has been seen walking through the graveyard, around the

Kirkton's gateway, c. 1900. Two ghostly monks have been seen through the right-hand arch.

east end of the cathedral, to an area still known as 'the monks' cemetery', where tradition has it they were buried. Just beyond this area are the ruined arches of the Infirmary, the monks' hospital from the days of the abbey. Built into the ruins are several flats; residents have told me that they sometimes look out on to the ruins at night to see the hooded figure of a monk gliding up and down, with a glowing lantern in his hand; perhaps the spectre of the monks' doctor checking on his patients?

We have even had sightings in the graveyard from people on the Peterborough Ghost Walk. Whilst on a walk on 30 October 2005, a lady and her grown-up daughter were the first into this area, before myself or the rest of the party, and swore that they had seen a white, female figure walking between the gravestones in the churchyard at speed. They initially thought it was something set up as part of the walk, but it was not. We checked and could find nothing there; both women were quite genuine and obviously much shaken by the experience.

Infirmary ruins, c. 1900. Residents living by the ruins today have seen a phantom monk in the area.

West Range Ghosts

Opposite the cathedral's spectacular West Front is another range of historic buildings. To the left is St Nicholas' Gateway, the Norman medieval archway into the precincts. To the right of this is the surviving east end of the Chapel of St Thomas Becket, built about 1174, where the abbey's extensive collection of holy relics was once kept. These included the arm of St Oswald, several pieces of the true cross, and the bloodied robes that Thomas Becket was wearing when murdered at Canterbury Cathedral in 1170. When Henry VIII dissolved the abbey and created the Diocese of Peterborough in 1541, he also created a grammar school for boys in the city, the King's School. The school remained in the precincts until 1885, when it moved to its current location on Park Road. The buildings to the right of the chapel were also connected to the school. The lovely range of brick Georgian houses was built around 1710, as lodgings for teachers and boarding students. Today it comprises flats for cathedral staff. One of its former residents was Canon E.G. Swain, sacrist and librarian for the cathedral, who published a volume of short ghost stories, *The Stoneground Ghost Tales*, in 1912. He was also a close friend of famed ghost story writer M.R. James.

The ghost of a little girl has been seen at a first-floor window of a house in Minster Precincts. She has been spotted on many occasions by local people or visitors to the precincts. A former gardener at the cathedral told me that he saw her on many occasions. She always appears sat just inside the window; a small girl aged seven or eight, with long dark hair and a pale-coloured Victorian dress. Who the girl is and why she haunts this window is unknown,

The West Range. The ghost of a little girl is said to appear in a window over the left-hand front door.

but she has not been seen by the residents inside the property.

One ghost that has been seen by residents in the top-floor flats is the dark figure of a man; he wears a cloak and a broad-brimmed hat, and appears on rare occasions, always just after midnight. He walks along the top floor of the houses, simply passing through a wall when he encounters one. One resident told me that they refer to him as 'Mr Sandeman', as he resembles the cloaked man on the front of a Sandeman port bottle!

Another ghostly monk is associated with the former Tourist Information Centre, in the cellars underneath the row of West Range houses. The centre was located in these wonderful brick-vaulted rooms until it relocated to its current site on Bridge Street in 2010. The women who worked there claimed that there was a mischievous ghost that they nicknamed 'Benedict'. When the centre was being installed in the late 1990s, workmen were rather astonished when the figure of the monk began appearing, on one occasion walking out of a wall right next to one of them! After this particular incident, the scared workmen became

so nervous of the apparition that they asked the then dean of Peterborough Cathedral to perform an exorcism. The dean simply told them to get on with the job!

The ladies from the Tourist Information Centre claimed that the mischievous monk often moved items about, pushing a mirror off a shelf in 2001, and on other occasions turning lights on and off. He also seems to have been caught short overnight – as despite having an all female staff, the women who worked there claimed to often find the seat mysteriously left up in their staff toilet when they arrived in the morning. Some of the staff just felt uncomfortable in the building, one telling me that when she went down the back corridor to the stockroom she often felt as though she was being followed, and a 'cold gripping fear' would come over her. One of her colleagues agreed with this view, saying that one Sunday morning she heard a loud bang from this corridor. When she got to the area, she 'felt too afraid to go further, felt cold, unsafe and had to get out', suddenly experiencing 'a real sense of panic and fear'. Fetching a colleague to back her up, they went into the corridor and could find no explanation for the sound. The same woman actually saw the ghost one morning. She rolled up the shutter and walked into the building only to find a semi-transparent figure, in a muddy brown monk's robe and hood, standing near the desk. As she stared at it the figure turned, walked into a wall and vanished.

This monk may migrate across the yard and into the Minster Precincts, just to the right of the Norman arch as you enter from Cathedral Square – either that or he has a similarly mischievous colleague. A few years ago, the building in question was occupied by a local firm of estate agents and solicitors. Several of them told me that they had witnessed the ghostly figure of a monk on the staircase, or sometimes upstairs in the room in which they kept their photocopier. One lady told me she thought he must have some kind of fascination for this particular device, given the number of times she saw him in there!

Oxney Grange

About a mile away from Flag Fen, on the back road into the village of Eye, is a gated premises converted from an old, stone farmhouse. This is Oxney Grange, the oldest parts of which date back to the Middle Ages.

At that time Oxney was a monastic farm, owned by Peterborough Abbey (today the cathedral). The farm produced food for the monks, the excess being sold off to generate funds for the abbey. In 1125 there were twenty-three cattle and a herder living on-site, but the place was expanded by the end of the century with a chapel being constructed. The medieval parts of the current building were probably built during an expansion of the site around 1320. After the dissolution of Peterborough Abbey, it became privately owned. Much of the current building dates to the nineteenth century, when it was substantially rebuilt. The house was abandoned in 1999 and damaged by fire in 2003. It has recently been restored and turned into luxury apartments. It is also said to be haunted.

Local legend has it that in the mid-1400s a group of young men had recently joined Peterborough Abbey as lay brothers – trainee monks. After some months of a vegetarian diet and having to get up at all hours of the day and night to go to church services, six of the young men were so fed up with their new chosen life and its discipline that they sneaked out of the abbey, into the town, and went to the pub. They enjoyed themselves so much that they carried on to another, then another …

They ended up very drunk and eventually staggered back to the abbey, singing loudly. This was not the sort of behaviour expected of monks, and the abbot was furious. The following morning, the hungover young men were summoned before him to get a thorough telling-off. As a penance, they were sent out to Oxney Grange for a month to do all the filthy jobs on the farm, such as mucking the cows out; so the six young men trudged out the three miles to Oxney. When they arrived, they found that they were on their own. The monk usually in charge of the farm had been taken ill and was absent, so the young men were left to their own devices. What did they do? Got drunk all over again. This time they got so paralytic that they got into an argument with each other. The argument developed into a fight, and two of the monks ended up dead.

Whilst this may be a legend, drunkenness was genuinely a problem at Oxney,

Oxney Grange.

41

with the Bishop of Lincoln being called in to investigate the dissolute lifestyle of the monks there in 1442. Four years later, the Abbot of Peterborough was exiled to Oxney after breaking his vow of chastity and having an affair with the wife of the park warden at Eyebury.

As a result of the alleged murders, the site is said to be cursed – haunted by two phantom monks (the ones who died, presumably), a White Lady and a Blue Lady, and a phantom dog. A headless horseman has been seen riding past, and there is something so unpleasant in the cellar that nobody will go down there. A local resident, Mr Carroll, who was brought up in the house in the 1950s, told me that neither he nor his mother would go down to the cellar for fear of what was there. He would only describe this as 'something awful in the cellar'. They kept trays of eggs on a shelf alongside the cellar, and if they ever pushed the trays too close to the cellar door, then eggs would fly off by themselves.

Some years ago, one former resident allegedly got rather a shock when she had a new bathroom installed in the Grange. The night after the bathroom was finished, she decided to have a luxurious soak in her new bath. She put in plenty of hot water with bubble bath, and settled into the water to enjoy a relaxing hour with a good book. She said that as soon as she sat down, in an instant the water went from piping hot to freezing cold, and she felt that there were pairs of invisible hands holding her there so she could not move, could not even scream. She was pinned for a few moments until the hands went away, at which point she couldn't get out of the bath fast enough. Funnily enough, the bath was never used again.

Black Shuck

One of the most notorious ghosts in the Peterborough area is that of the demon hellhound, Black Shuck. Shuck or Scucca is an Anglo-Saxon word meaning demon or devil.

Phantom dogs are common in English folklore; there are many well-known examples across the country. The Barghest, for example, is said to haunt the North York Moors between York and Whitby. When Bram Stoker heard the story whilst staying on holiday in Whitby in the 1880s, he incorporated it into his novel, *Dracula*. In the book, the great vampire comes ashore at Whitby from the wrecked ship *Demeter* in the form of a great, black dog.

The largest and most unpleasant of all the black dogs in the British Isles is Black Shuck. Various parts of East Anglia lay claim to him – including parts of Norfolk, and Bungay in Suffolk, where it is said that marks were left on the church door by Shuck attempting to claw his way in. Some claim that these stories go back to Viking legends of black dogs used by the pagan gods; others claim that they were established more recently by smugglers in the fens, to keep the unwary from prying into their business at night by frightening them away. The earliest documented version of the story comes from Peterborough and dates back to 1127.

In the chronicles of the time, it was said that the Abbot of Peterborough, a Frenchman called Henry d'Angély, was a rather godless and worldly man. He planned to loot Peterborough of its wealth and run away with it back to France. His own monks so despised him that they started praying to the Almighty to do something about him. Unfortunately, their prayers were answered; a case of 'be careful what you wish for'.

Gravestones in the cathedral graveyard.

heard at night during the whole of lent, throughout the woodland and plains, from the monastery as far as Stamford. For there appeared, as it were, hunters with horns and hounds, all being jet black, their horses and hounds as well, and some rode as it were on goats and had great eyes and there were twenty or thirty together. And this is no false tale, for many men of faithful report both saw them and heard the horns. (*Peterborough Chronicle of Hugh Candidus*)

It was said by some local people that one hound, Shuck, remained as an eternal warning never to let an evil man take over the abbey again …

Shuck is described as being huge, black and hairy, with red eyes that weep fire – and is a harbinger of death; anyone who sees him will be dead by sunrise. Most sightings of him were on the fen roads between Peterborough and Whittlesey or Wisbech. In one case in Tudor Peterborough, this black dog entered two churches a few miles apart and killed several members of the congregation by the 'wringing of necks'! He was last seen in the 1920s, but that doesn't mean he won't be seen again.

In 1901, Sir Arthur Conan Doyle was on a golfing holiday at Cromer, in Norfolk, when he heard the story of Black Shuck. He was so fascinated that he wrote it into his next Sherlock Holmes novel, mixed in with another holiday in Devon and the name of a friend's manservant, Mr Baskerville. Black Shuck was thus transformed into one of Holmes' most famous adversaries – the Hound of the Baskervilles.

A dread portent followed, warning the people and monks of Peterborough about tolerating such a godless man in a godly role. Each night, during the fast of Lent, a demonic 'wild hunt' was sent to terrorise the area. The *Peterborough Chronicle* (part of the Anglo-Saxon Chronicle, much of which was written at Peterborough Abbey) describes it thus:

In the very year in which he came to the abbey, marvellous portents were seen and

3

Military Ghosts

PETERBOROUGH may be a peace-ful place today, but that has not always been the case. The city has a proud military heritage – dating back over 2,000 years to the establishment of a huge Roman fortress in the area, and continuing today with RAF Wittering. The association with many conflicts over the centuries has left its own ghostly imprint upon the area.

Roman Remains

The Romans first arrived in the Peterborough area in AD 43, during the early stages of their invasion. It took the Roman legions over thirty years to pacify the British provinces; during this period, the area remained a militarised zone, with a substantial fortress (built under what is today Longthorpe golf course) to house part of the 9th Legion (famed as the alleged 'lost legion' of film and novels), with a subsidiary fort at Water Newton to control a river crossing.

It is known that the 9th Legion marched out of the area to try to quell the rising by the native Iceni tribe and Queen Boudica in AD 60. These soldiers were ambushed by Boudica's tribesmen and massacred, according to the Roman historian Tacitus; archaeological evidence from Longthorpe indicates hasty defences on a much smaller scale erected within the fort, which suggests that the survivors holed up there after this initial military disaster. The Roman legions finally defeated Boudica and order was restored. Although the military moved on from the area around Peterborough, a township had sprung up around the fort at Water Newton. This became the Roman town of Durobrivae, a substantial walled town made wealthy by the rich farmland around it and the local production of distinctive brown pottery, known today as 'Nene Valley Ware', which is found on sites across Britain.

Ghostly Roman soldiers have been seen at a number of places around the city. To the east, in the district of Paston, runs a surviving section of Car Dyke. This substantial earthwork and drainage ditch ran for many miles, and archaeologists debate its purpose: perhaps an attempt at fen drainage; a form of canal; a boundary marker; or a statement of Roman imperial power. Local people have claimed to see ghostly figures, identifiable as Roman soldiers, at night on the earthwork.

Romans at the Peterborough Heritage Festival. Sites in the area are haunted by Roman soldiers. (Courtesy of IX Legion Hispania/Roman Military Research Society)

one wall of the living room, march across the room and then disappear through the opposite wall. They are, however, only visible from the waist up. This may be because the original Roman surface is below the current floor, as with the ghostly monk in the cathedral (*see* Chapter Two). The lady of the house told me that trying to watch *Eastenders* on television through the ghostly figures really puts her off – although her husband was of the opinion that seeing the soldiers was preferable to watching the soap opera!

Civil War Ghosts

Built in the thirteenth century as a fortified manor house, Woodcroft Castle near Helpston is today a private house. It is also home to one of the area's most gruesome and well-known ghosts, said to be that of Dr Michael Hudson, resident in the house at the time of the English Civil War.

Dr Hudson was not a medical doctor, but a priest. He had been parish priest at Uffington, but when Civil War erupted in 1642 he went to Oxford – the Royalist capital throughout the war – and became chaplain to Charles I. In 1646, Hudson was with King Charles when he spent his last night of freedom at Stamford on 3 May, prior to his surrendering to the Scots. The Scots promptly sold the monarch to Parliament and Charles was imprisoned in the rooms over the cathedral gateway in Peterborough on his way south. When war reignited in 1648, Hudson acted as the Royalist Scoutmaster-General (effectively their intelligence chief) and garrisoned Woodcroft (a large, stone house with a tower at one end, surrounded by a water-filled moat) with Cavalier soldiers. In June he had been trying to foment a rising against

Near the village of Alwalton and the East of England Showground is a business park, one of the main units of which is occupied by a publishing company called Bauer (formerly Emap), which is responsible for producing many of the best-known magazines you will find in your local newsagent. Various staff who have worked there believe that the building is haunted, despite being relatively modern. Lights and doors seem sometimes to have a mind of their own, and it is even claimed that two shadowy figures on horseback have been seen in one part of the building. When one considers that archaeologists had to clear Roman and Anglo-Saxon burials when these buildings were built, this is perhaps less surprising.

To the west of the city, outside the village of Helpston, local people have allegedly seen Roman cavalry riding across the fields; whilst at a modern bungalow to the south at Orton Longueville, the residents claim to have a very close relationship with their resident Romans. Soldiers emerge from

Woodcroft Castle. (From The Victoria History of the County of Northamptonshire, *1902)*

the victorious Parliamentarians in Stamford, only to be driven out. He was pursued back to Woodcroft by a troop of soldiers led by Captain William Smart. The Roundheads attempted to storm the castle, only to be driven off with the loss of several men, including Smart himself.

Within hours, a full regiment of Roundhead soldiers arrived as reinforcements. They were led by Captain Smart's brother-in-law Colonel Winters – who was now out for vengeance, but began by summoning Dr Hudson to surrender. What happened next is reminiscent of a Monty Python film, as Dr Hudson climbed onto the top of the castle's tower to shout down his answer, effectively telling them to get lost. Again they asked him to give up, pointing out that the king had already been captured and the war was effectively over. Again, Hudson refused, so the Roundheads attacked the castle. After several hours attempting to break in, the Roundheads withdrew. They again attempted to get Hudson to surrender, saying that if they were forced to storm the castle they would give no quarter and kill everyone they found inside. Hudson still refused.

Again the Roundheads attacked. During the assault, Hudson stood on his tower

shouting encouragement to his own men and hurling abuse at his enemies. He then got rather a shock when the gate was blown in by his enemies using a petard, a gun-powder-packed bomb placed against the castle gates. As the only way out was being stormed, Dr Hudson attempted to avoid being hacked to pieces by dangling from the ramparts. He was found by Roundhead soldiers, who cut off his hands, causing him to plunge into the moat below – a genuine case of 'look, no hands'!

Hudson somehow managed to swim across the moat (how he did this with no hands is unclear), only to be dragged out by two vengeful soldiers. One, called Egborough, was the former servant to the parish priest at Castor and the other, Walker, was a 'low-born shopkeeper from Stamford' (according to a contemporary account). Dr Hudson was disembowelled by the men with a halberd, and had his tongue ripped out (in retribution for the insults he had hurled from the ramparts). At this point he finally expired. The grisly relic of his tongue was dried and paraded around local towns and villages, both as a trophy and as a warning against anyone else who dared use their wagging tongues to insult the Roundheads.

There are two spooky codas to this story. Firstly, it was rumoured that the two men who finally mutilated and killed Dr Hudson died under mysterious circumstances, cursed for having killed him. Secondly, Hudson's gruesome death is said to be annually re-enacted in spectral form; those who gather by the moat late at night (particularly on 6 June, the anniversary of his death) might see a ghastly apparition emerge from the waters: the ghostly figure of a man, wet, bloody and muddy, with no hands. On other nights his ghostly screams have been heard by witnesses. There are other ghosts said to lurk in the castle, including a phantom nun, but it is Dr Hudson's tragic story that captures the imagination and chills the blood.

Woodcroft is not the only place in the area where ghostly Civil War soldiers have been seen. Villagers in Elton, to the west of Peterborough, claim that the back road to the city, the Chesterton road, is haunted by phantoms of the period – although whether they are Roundheads or Cavaliers is unknown. Similarly mysterious is the reason why they haunt this specific road, given that no fighting is documented to have taken place here. Reports indicate that they are seasonal apparitions, only manifesting between the beginning of January and the end of March. The soldiers have been seen in some numbers, either camped in fields close to the junction leading to the village of Great Gidding, or on the road with dozens of men, pikemen and musketeers, fully equipped and marching in column. One lady, who lives on the edge of Elton, told me that she regularly hears the eerie sound of military drums going past her cottage in the winter months; another woman told me that she has seen the ghostly soldiers so often that she always drives down that road at that time of year – whilst keeping to the middle, so as to avoid running the soldiers over!

Napoleonic Hauntings

If you approach Peterborough from the south-west, along the A15 near Yaxley, you will pass a rather curious memorial which marks an internationally significant site. To the left-hand side of the road is a stone column with a bronze eagle perched on the top, a memorial to the prisoners-of-war kept 200 years ago in the field behind – the site of the world's first purpose-built prisoner-of-war camp. This camp, the Norman Cross Depot, was designed to house French prisoners taken in the wars against Napoleon.

The Napoleonic Wars lasted from 1793 until 1814 (with brief interludes of peace). Throughout these wars, Britain was the only country which remained steadfastly at war with Revolutionary and Napoleonic France – a war we were able to sustain through the economic power of the nascent British Empire, a well-trained and successful army under the Duke of Wellington, and above all the might of the Royal Navy in the age of Nelson. The navy was so successful against the French fleet that many enemy ships and thousands of sailors were captured. The problem was what to do with these captured servicemen.

Initially, the British government reverted to its tried and tested solution of putting prisoners-of-war in old castles across the country, or prison hulks (decommissioned warships) moored in rivers. As the war progressed, these solutions proved inadequate, so in 1797 a camp was built at Norman Cross near Peterborough, the first such

The storming of Woodcroft Castle. Dr Hudson can be seen dangling from the tower. (From Desiderata Curiosa, Vol. II, by Francis Peck, 1735)

The eagle memorial at Norman Cross.

men from other nations allied to Napoleon – there were Dutch, German, Italian and Polish men, even a few Americans by the end of the war. The youngest of them was ten years old.

Conditions inside may seem harsh by modern standards, but seemed positively enlightened at the time. The prisoners were clothed (in yellow uniforms to aid detection in case of escape), reasonably well fed, and encouraged to make crafts – principally bone or straw decorative items – which they could then sell to local people at a market by the east gate of the camp once a month. Many examples of these beautiful items can be seen on display at Peterborough Museum. Even so, there were attempts to escape, using such ruses as digging a tunnel, disguising oneself as one of the soldiers guarding the camp, or forming a human battering ram to force down the wall. A few prisoners escaped successfully, most were recaptured, and a few were killed during their attempt. Other prisoners died of disease – over 1,200 in a bad typhoid outbreak in 1807, and perhaps 400 more overall. Most were buried in grave pits around the camp, and a few were buried in local parish graveyards at Yaxley and Stilton. The camp was closed in 1814 when Napoleon abdicated for the first time, and the prisoners were sent home. The site was dismantled and the materials sold off in 1816.

Today, only a couple of buildings survive from the camp, and are now private residences. The site of the camp itself is now farmland, although the earthworks and ditches can be clearly seen. Ghostly echoes of the camp at Norman Cross do remain. Some claim that the site has never been built over due to a local belief that it was cursed by the men who died there – although it is perhaps for the more practical

camp of its kind anywhere, at any time. The site was picked as it was well-wooded and watered, and had good transport links to bring in the prisoners, supplies and troops. It was also thought to be far enough inland and away from any unfortified ports to make escape back to France difficult. The camp occupied some 40 acres, was built mostly of timber (it was only ever intended to be temporary), and housed 7,000 prisoners plus 1,000 British soldiers or militia as guards. When one bears in mind that the population of Peterborough at this time was about 3,500, the camp had a massive impact on the local economy. The prisoners were mostly French, but also included

reason that the massive ditches on the site would make building difficult; additionally, it is now a Scheduled Ancient Monument. More believable are the hauntings in the hotel to the west of the site, the Premier Inn at Norman Cross. Former staff have told me that there are a number of rooms on the camp-facing side where shadowy figures have been seen and unexplained temperature drops felt.

Curiously, there are related hauntings in the city centre. On Bridge Street, just opposite the Town Hall, is the Peterborough branch of WHSmith. This 1970s' building occupies the site of the former Angel Hotel – a coaching inn and one of Peterborough's longest-lived drinking establishments. There was once a tavern on this site called the Angel, dating back to the Middle Ages, which was owned by the abbey (hence its name). In 1483 the landlord paid 60s in rent to the monastery (indicating that it was a profitable establishment), whilst by the Tudor period it was famed for cock-

fighting and bear-baiting in the yard at the back. The building that many Peterborians remember is the Georgian rebuild of the inn; it was in the yard of this establishment that a French prisoner being taken under guard to Norman Cross was shot dead, whilst trying to escape, on 4 February 1808. Staff who work at WHSmith have told me that things have unaccountably moved around in the shop, ghostly footsteps have been heard and cold spots felt. Whether these phenomena are connected to the unsuccessful French escapee or to another part of the Angel's long history is unclear.

More strange, perhaps, is the soldier said to haunt the Key Theatre near the Embankment. There is a long tradition in this country of theatrical hauntings, and it is an unusual theatre that does not have at least one ghost story. The Key may seem rather too modern to have any hauntings – it only opened to the public in 1973 – but there are said to be two spirits in its premises. Staff and guest artists (and even a

Town bridge, c. 1890. Prisoners for Norman Cross were unloaded from barges near here.

former theatre cat) have seen the ghost of a little girl in the corridor underneath the main stage; her story is unknown. The other spirit appears to be that of a redcoat soldier, who has been picked up on by several mediums over the years, and is apparently associated with dressing room No. 1. Is this ghost somehow connected to the detachments of prisoners destined for Norman Cross, guarded by redcoats from the British army, who would have disembarked from barges just yards away?

Westwood Airfield

The East of England is very flat and is also the part of the country closest to Germany. As such, during the Second World War it was covered with airfields – on average one every seven miles. A number of these were around Peterborough; most are now long gone, although the echoes of some survive. There are few airfield sites across the UK that cannot boast at least one ghost story, and the site of the former RAF Peterborough in no exception.

The Westwood area of the city, now covered by housing estates, was once the base of RAF Peterborough. Back in the 1920s there were plans to establish a municipal airport on this site, but in the event the RAF opened a base primarily for aircraft storage in 1932. It was then used as a training base for pilots – teaching navigation, amongst other things, from 1935 until 1948. American servicemen were stationed at the airfield during the war; post-war French airmen were also trained there. Although the base was not used for operational missions, some fifty accidents occurred during training. Some of these resulted in fatalities, including a serious crash in 1936 when four men were killed. The airfield was also bombed several times during the war. After 1948 a helicopter service ran from the site, and the Air Training Corps continued to use the station. In more recent times, the base has been redeveloped as housing estates and industrial parks. It is said that ghostly vestiges of the airfield remain.

The former officers' mess still stands on Cottesmore Close, and at one time was used as Peterborough City Council's training centre. Staff there reported seeing a ghostly pilot on the first floor. Residents on Savile Road, where the station's offices and sergeants' mess used to be, have also seen a phantom airman. One lady who lives on that road stopped me after a ghost walk, telling me that she regularly hears the sound of footsteps – military hobnailed boots on a wooden floor, despite the fact that she has no such flooring in her property. Another couple in the area say that they have heard the sounds of phantom aircraft passing overhead, and have even seen the landing lights on the undercarriage shining in through their bedroom curtains. Obviously no aircraft lands in Westwood now, but where their house stands today was where the runway was seventy years ago.

Hauntings have peaked in the area several times over the years, leading to coverage in the local media. The *Peterborough Standard* of 27 October 1972 reported paranormal occurrences in Ravensthorpe, an area built on part of the old Westwood site. In the article, the local vicar, Jeffrey Bell, described the hauntings as '… very serious. Many people on the estate are upset and disturbed'. He believed there was a pattern to the hauntings, saying:

> At Swanspool they seemed always to occur about 3 a.m.; in White Cross at 1 a.m. Something seems to be moving across the estate. I have no idea what

The officers' mess building, RAF Westwood. A phantom pilot has been seen in this building.

causes it. Places seem to carry with them events and pick up things that happen in the past.

Mr John Embry, a resident in White Cross, was quoted as saying: 'I laughed when the noises and things first started, but now I defy anyone to deny that there is a ghost or poltergeist in this house.' His neighbour, Linda Gardner, told the newspaper: 'I quite often hear a noise in the bedroom as if someone is marching about in hobnailed boots. I rush upstairs and there's no one there.'

Another bout of hauntings on the former airfield made front page headlines for the *Peterborough Evening Telegraph* of 7 October 1998. An unnamed family in Westwood was reported as having been terrified by the appearances of a ghostly airman in their property over a two-year period, despite at least two apparently unsuccessful attempts to have the house exorcised. The father gave a description of the ghost:

I woke up one night to see a figure standing by the window. I thought I was dreaming; I could not make it out clearly. He was about thirty years old and was wearing a bluey-black airman's uniform. He walked straight by me. I didn't know why but I followed him. He walked down the stairs and when he got to the front door he disappeared. I wasn't scared, but it worried my wife. And when the noises and strange things continued, we got an exorcist in.

It would seem that the site of the former airfield has more that just memories …

RAF Wittering

To the north of Peterborough, just off the A1 on the way to Stamford, is RAF Wittering: one of the oldest such stations in the country. It was established in 1916 as a fighter station for the Royal Flying Corps, to provide cover against Zeppelin raids on the region. It was closed in 1920, and then reopened in 1924 as a flight training school for the RAF. In 1938 it became a fighter base, with Spitfires and Hurricanes operating from there throughout the Battle of Britain. The base was bombed by the Luftwaffe on at least five occasions – the heaviest attack, in March 1941, resulting in the deaths of seventeen servicemen. The base also played host to American aircrews during the war, and had a special unit for testing captured German aircraft. Post-war, the station has been used as a training base again – as a home for the British nuclear deterrent during the 1950s and '60s, and, until recently, as the 'home

of the Harrier', the iconic vertical takeoff and landing aircraft.

Although the Harriers have now left, Wittering is still an operational military base complete with ghost stories. Those working in the control tower claim to have seen the ghostly figure of a wartime pilot walking around the building, and even climbing into the tower itself. Security guards are nervous about going near hangar No. 1 – and not just the men but also their fierce Alsatian guard dogs. These dogs whimper and cower when taken near the building, as if they can sense another ghostly pilot in residence there. One soldier stationed at Wittering described to me a frightening experience he'd had whilst on guard duty one night. On patrol with a colleague, he went past some portable offices (used by bomb disposal teams) which were adjacent to hangar No. 1. They noticed, through the window, that a light was on inside one of the offices. As they approached, they heard the radio on inside – despite the fact that

The Harrier on 'gate guard' outside RAF Wittering. The airfield has several ghosts.

Peterscourt; ghostly music has been heard inside.

it was late at night and there should be nobody in there. When they got to the door to investigate, they heard the radio switch off. They opened the door to find nobody inside; there was no way out of the room other than the doorway they were standing in. He told me that at this point they turned the light off, locked the door and walked away as quickly as possible.

American Pilots in Peterscourt

It is not just British pilots who haunt the area. During the war, Peterborough was surrounded by American airbases at villages such as Polebrook, King's Cliffe and Glatton. From these bases, American crews would fly out on daylight raids over Germany in their huge B-17 bomber aircraft, many of them never to return. On their nights off, the young Americans lived it up in Peterborough, drinking in the local pubs and meeting some of the local ladies – 'overpaid, oversexed and over 'ere'. The most famous of these Americans was the Hollywood film star Clark Gable, who did his wartime service in 1943 at RAF Polebrook, and apparently spent much of his time being chased around the city streets by adoring young ladies!

The Americans took over the Peterscourt building in the heart of the city centre for their own purposes. This gothic brick edifice still stands on Midgate, opposite the market, today. It was built in 1859 as a teacher training college, designed by George Gilbert Scott – best known as the designer of St Pancras station. During the war, the American servicemen used the building as a social club and dance hall known as the American Red Cross Club. Today the building is used for offices, and many of those who work inside claim to have heard phantom footsteps and even the ghostly sounds of Big Band music (the likes

Evening Telegraph *building. The phantom couple appear by the hedge in the middle of the picture.*

of Glenn Miller). Are these the ghosts of the young Americans who lost their lives? Are they coming back for one last dance?

A Wartime Couple in Priestgate

Another paranormal account related to Peterborough's wartime story is located on Priestgate, outside the building which is home to the *Peterborough Evening Telegraph*. One hot, sunny day in June 2000, at around 9.30 a.m., a local chap called Tony came into the city centre to see his solicitor. He parked his car just around the corner, opposite the steps into the *Evening Telegraph* building, with the front of the car facing up towards Cowgate. He got out of his car, got a ticket from the parking machine, and then got back into the driver's seat to put the ticket in the windscreen. As he glanced back up, he was astonished to see two

people apparently appear out of thin air at the end of the hedge to the right of the steps. He was further surprised to see that, on such a hot day, they were both wearing heavy winter overcoats. He described them as being a man and a woman in their mid-twenties, dressed in 1930s'-style clothing, both with heavy overcoats and hats. The man was wearing a trilby and carrying a briefcase. They were arm-in-arm, chatting away, and walked up to the end of the street, where they seemed to vanish by a hedge at the end of Cowgate. He said that, apart from their old-fashioned dress and the fact that they appeared and disappeared into thin air, they seemed just like living, breathing people.

Not only is the witness very credible and detailed in his description, he is not the only person to have seen this couple. Another witness gave an identical description of a sighting five years later, completely independently, but with the additional detail that the couple were wearing cardboard gas mask boxes. Who this young couple are is unknown; Peterborough was incredibly lucky and suffered only a few civilian deaths from enemy bombing during the war – a young couple was not amongst those casualties. Where they appear corresponds exactly to where an alley was seventy years ago, between some railway cottages that stood on the site; this perhaps explains why they appear where they do. Perhaps they are simply a 'stone tape' recording (*see* Afterword) of two young people who took that route every day during those stressful times, and have left a distant memory of their passing.

4

Railway-Related Ghosts

ONE of the key turning points in Peterborough's story was the coming of the railways in 1845 – the catalyst for turning a small market town into the city that we have today. Contrary to popular myth, Stamford was not offered the railway line first only to turn it down; Peterborough was chosen as a railway centre over its northern neighbour because it was easier, from an engineering perspective, to build the line through. The first railway line to come through the town was to Northampton (now defunct, although a section survives as the Nene Valley Railway), with a terminus at Peterborough East station which stood on the south bank of the river. By 1850, Peterborough North station had been added at the site of the current station, to service the needs of the railway line from London to York, today the East Coast main line.

The city expanded on the back of the railway boom, from a population of 3,500 in 1840 to some 35,000 in 1900. These were not just workers for the railways; the trains had a knock-on effect on other industries. Brick-making had been going on for centuries in the area, but the railways allowed mass production and export for the first time, making Fletton bricks famous the world over. A skilled engineering workforce developed in the city as the railways encouraged other companies, such as Baker Perkins and Peter Brotherhood, to establish themselves here. A Large number of people still depend on the railway in Peterborough, particularly as the town is a commutable distance to London.

Given the importance of the railways, and the fact that they have caused accidents and fatalities, it is not surprising to find that Peterborough also has some railway-related ghosts.

The Lady on the Durham Train

One of the most famous railway hauntings connected with Peterborough – told many times in various compendiums of ghost stories – is the rather odd case of the lady on the Durham train. The story goes back to the autumn of 1945, shortly after the end of the Second World War, and concerns a Mr and Mrs Whishart. This couple lived in North London, but decided to take a few days away to visit relatives in Newcastle. They duly took the 10.30 a.m. train from

Peterborough railway station is on the left, where a ghostly figure got on the Durham train. To the right is the Great Northern Hotel, haunted by a phantom waiter who committed suicide in the building.

The railway bridge over the River Nene; built in 1850, this is the oldest iron railway bridge in Britain.

King's Cross one weekday morning to head north, stocked up with a pile of newspapers to keep themselves occupied on the long journey. By good fortune they were able to find an empty Second Class compartment and thus have the journey to themselves – until the train eventually passed the chimneys of the Fletton brickworks that announced they were pulling into Peterborough North station.

After a few minutes of bustling outside the carriage, the train was ready to depart. Just as it was about to pull out of Peterborough, the door to the Wisharts' compartment opened and an elderly lady walked in wearing a black silk dress and black hat, both very old-fashioned and Victorian in style. She was carrying a large wicker basket with a white linen top, again very old-fashioned. The lady nodded and smiled at the Wisharts, sat down opposite them, and seemed lost in her own thoughts. Other than noting the quality and style of the lady's dress, and smiling companionably back at her, the Wisharts returned to their newspapers. There was no conversation in the carriage, and indeed Mr Wishart soon dozed off and started to snore quite loudly.

He was jolted awake as the train then pulled into Grantham. Mrs Wishart whispered to her husband that she really fancied a cup of tea, so he got up to get one from the station tea room before the train moved on again. As he left the carriage, he politely asked the old lady in black if she would also like a cup of tea, and she nodded her acceptance. Just as the train was about to leave, Mr Wishart returned with three paper cups of tea. The old lady took one and murmured her thanks.

The train continued north – the old lady sitting quietly with her eyes closed, and the Wisharts reading the news and occasionally glancing curiously at the old lady.

Eventually the train pulled into Durham station and the old lady got up to leave. Mr Wishart politely gave her a hand down onto the platform. As she stepped out and took her basket from him, the lady said, 'I wish you many happy years.' To his astonishment, she then vanished into thin air; he looked around but could find no trace of her anywhere. He staggered back into the carriage to tell his wife what had happened, half wondering if he had imagined the old lady from the start, only to see the full, cold cup of tea he had given her still standing on the table in the carriage.

Ghosts in the Railway Yards

Railways can be dangerous places and accidents, sometimes fatal, have been known to happen. Over the last 150 years, a number of railway workers have been badly injured in the complex of railway sidings and works around Peterborough. In 1898 Jack Binns, famed as a heroic radio operator in the merchant navy (in 1909 he sent the first ever SOS telegraph), was badly injured and almost crippled by a railway engine in the Peterborough yards. Others have been even less fortunate, such as railwayman George Ruff, who was killed in the yards on 16 January 1941 by a German bomb.

Stories of paranormal occurrences in the railway yards have circulated amongst railway workers past and present; possibly the phenomena are the result of past accidents. One shed – used for storage and as an occasional staffroom by railway workers – has a rather sinister reputation. Workers sheltering in there at night have found that the door can sometimes become undone and start slamming backwards and forwards by itself, even when there is no wind and the door has been firmly latched. On other occasions there have been reports of some-one banging on the walls outside, almost as if they were doing so with a hammer, but upon investigation there has been no sign of anybody there. One railway worker told me that this had happened to him and a colleague a few years ago, and, as a result, both of them refused to ever set foot in the building thereafter.

Conington Crossing

One particular accident black spot on the railway around Peterborough is the level crossing over the East Coast line, just out-side the village of Conington. For years there was a stream of accidents and fatalities at this site, largely because the road there is very narrow, the view of the line restricted, and the gates were operated manually by members of the public – many of whom took unnecessary risks when crossing the busy line. Even though the railway compa-nies put up signs warning people about the dangers, accidents still happened.

At 7 a.m. on 30 April 1945, a lorry carry-ing German prisoners-of-war from Glatton camp (to work on nearby farms) was going across the Conington crossing in thick fog – with visibility down to fifteen yards, according to an account in the *Peterborough Citizen* – only to be hit side-on by a railway engine. Six of the German prisoners were killed; five more were injured and taken to the hospital in Peterborough. To add to the carnage, a lorry carrying the injured away from the crossing then hit a bus in the fog, badly injuring two more people in the process.

The most famous death at the crossing is that of Arthur Mellows, solicitor, educa-tionalist, city councillor, former Mayor of Peterborough, and commanding officer of

Conington level crossing, where a ghostly black car has been seen.

the local Home Guard during the war. He is commemorated today by the local school in Glinton named in his honour. On 16 October 1948, at about 5.30 p.m., Mellows was driving home in his large black Chrysler car, accompanied by his faithful Labrador dog and his friend Mr Percival, after a day's shooting in the nearby woods. As they reached Conington, Mellows noticed a train standing some 200 yards to the south of the crossing, obviously awaiting a signal change to proceed north. Mr Percival got out of the car and opened the gates, and Mellows started to drive over the crossing. Mellows was concentrating so much on the train to the south that he failed to notice an express train from the north, which ploughed into the car, killing him and his dog. The dog was later buried by the crossing.

For many years thereafter there was a signal box at Conington. One of the duties of the signalmen was to open the gates at the crossing, in an effort to make the crossing safer. Many of the signalmen had odd experiences, and some eventually refused to work there. Some heard the gates apparently opening and closing by themselves – even though they were locked and there was nobody there. Others claim to have seen a large black car, such as that owned by Arthur Mellows, pull up at the gate, only to disappear when they went down to let it across. Although the signal box was closed in the 1970s and automatic gates were installed at Conington crossing, local people still claim that a phantom black car has been seen there – and they think twice about using the crossing at night.

Nene Valley Railway

One of Peterborough's most popular tourist attractions is Nene Valley Railway, which runs roughly eight miles from the edge of the city centre to a visitor centre at Wansford station near Stibbington, then on to Yarwell Tunnel. The railway line stopped carrying passenger traffic in 1966 and closed in 1972; however, this section was reopened as a visitor attraction in 1974 by a group of enthusiasts, supported by the Peterborough Development Corporation. Today the railway gets many thousands of visitors, not least families who come to see Thomas the Tank Engine, or take part in the Christmas 'Santa Specials'. Even people who have never visited Peterborough may be familiar with the railway, as it is a popular location for film and television productions, including two James Bond films, a version of *Murder on the Orient Express* and even a video for the rock band Queen!

The site also has its own ghost stories to tell, one particularly haunted area being the Yarwell Tunnel. The tunnel was built in 1845 by Irish navvies. They cut the tunnel using a combination of hand tools and explosives, and then used local clay to make bricks with which to line it. Drunkenness was rife, fights common, and accidents often took place – at least ten men died during the construction of the tunnel as a result. It is said that their ghosts still haunt the site; many people working in or near the tunnel claim to have heard odd noises, agonised cries, loud bangs or the sounds of men fighting. Tools left out during maintenance work have mysteriously gone missing, and, on one occasion some forty years ago, workmen narrowly avoided being run down by a train. The man left out on watch, whose job was to warn them of an approaching train, was found unconscious – knocked out, so he claimed, by 'someone he couldn't see'.

Another ghostly resident of Yarwell Tunnel is Snowy the cat. Snowy was the

Wansford station, Nene Valley Railway. The buildings in the background are where a ghostly passenger has been reported.

distinctive white pet cat of the station master of Wansford station back in the 1920s, and a familiar sight to everyone in the area. One day Snowy went missing, so his owner went out to find him. He eventually located the lost feline sitting on the sleepers between the tracks at the entrance to the Yarwell Tunnel. The station master went to retrieve Snowy, who promptly wandered off the rails again. Sadly the man must have been somewhat deaf, as when he stood on the tracks cursing the contrary cat he failed to notice a train which came out of the tunnel, hitting him and killing him instantly. The cat was unharmed, yet it is not the station master who haunts the area, but Snowy. Nene Valley Railway staff and visitors claim to have seen a white cat wandering around the entrance to the Yarwell Tunnel, mewing piteously, despite the fact that nobody local owns such a cat.

More recently, groups of ghost-hunters have turned their attention to Wansford station itself. The old station building on Platform 3, currently awaiting restoration, is said to be haunted by a phantom passenger. Doors have been heard opening and closing by themselves, caused by an entity

stomping round the station – presumably still waiting for a long-delayed train.

The Mayor's Walk Poltergeist

One of the most curious ghost stories in the area – and an example of that (thankfully) rarest of paranormal phenomena, the poltergeist – concerns a family of railway workers who lived in a railway cottage on Mayor's Walk. The case was faithfully documented in some detail by a local newspaper, the *Peterborough Advertiser*, in its edition on Saturday, 9 January 1892. It is from this account that the following story has been taken.

The story featured the Rimes family, who originally came from Crowland but had moved to Peterborough when Mr Rimes got a job with the Midland Railway. They lodged on Rogers Street, before taking the lease on No. 22 Mayor's Walk in the summer of 1891. The family consisted of Mr and Mrs Rimes and their three sons, two of whom were teenagers. The rent on the house was £12 a year, a reasonably large sum in those days, so they took in two lodgers – Mrs Rimes' brother and brother-in-law, Mr Want and Mr Easy, who also worked for the Midland Railway. The property had three bedrooms upstairs, joined by a corridor which led to a staircase. The front bedroom was occupied by Mr Want and one of the boys, the middle room by Mr Easy and the other two boys, and the back bedroom by Mr and Mrs Rimes.

Shortly after the family moved into the property, they began to be disturbed by the sound of someone banging at the front door late at night. Whenever they went to answer it, nobody was there. They assumed this was local children playing pranks on the new neighbours, and duly ignored it. Then, one night in early November, the family woke up as 'an unnatural wind' gusted through the top of the house and blew all the covers off the beds. They rationalised this as being a freak weather effect through an open window, but then the following night the knocking started.

Each night thereafter, at varying times of the night, there would be knocking, rapping, tapping and banging sounds out in the corridor. Whenever anyone got up to investigate, the noises would stop; by the time they reached the corridor there would be no sign of anyone there. Each night the noises got worse. The newspaper account describes them as sounding like they were …

… generally preceded by the booming of a telegraph wire … at intervals there would appear to be the tramp of a heavy tread, heavier … than anyone in the house could make along the passage, the wall would echo with an unearthly thumping, the bedroom doors would shake as if the house would be shaken down … on one occasion the violence was such that the handle was shaken from a door.

After a week or so of this, Mr Want repositioned his bed in a way that enabled him to leave the door open, remain in bed and keep watch – perhaps he was expecting to see one of the boys causing the noises. That night the sounds carried on unabated, but Mr Want could see no apparent reason for them. The house had no cellar and no attic and, despite wall panels being taken off and floorboards lifted, no explanation for the sounds could be found. The noises were now so loud that by Christmas the residents in the cottages adjoining the haunted property – No. 21, occupied by a train driver called Butler; and No. 23, occupied by a train guard called Goode – were also being kept awake.

A few nights before New Year, Messrs Want and Easy were anaesthetising themselves against the coming night of unnatural noises by drinking heavily in a local pub, when they met a fellow railway worker, Arthur Wilson. Wilson claimed to be something of an amateur ghost-hunter, and over a few drinks they told him their story. He offered to come and act as 'detective'.

On 29 December, Wilson stayed with the family – going upstairs with them when they retired as usual, expecting yet another sleepless night. After some time, the

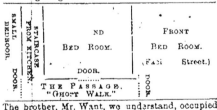

Peterborough Advertiser, *9 January 1892 – covering the hauntings at Mayor's Walk.*

61

A cottage on Mayor's Walk. It was in a house like this that the Rimes family suffered the terrible hauntings of 1891.

heard a huge crash from behind him, which he described as sounding like a 'huge sack of coals toppled pell-mell down the stairs'. The neighbours also heard this noise, saying later that it sounded like a cannon going off, and stating that they were in fear of No. 22 collapsing. At this point the banging started again, causing Wilson and the family to flee downstairs to the kitchen and huddle around the fire with the lights on – until dawn, when the disturbances stopped.

A rather scared and mystified Wilson left the house the following morning; one suspects he never went ghost-hunting again. The Rimes family packed their bags and moved out a few days later, to a house in Monument Street. The haunted house is still there today, although it is no longer No. 22 as the street has been renumbered. To preserve the current occupants from the curious, I shall not reveal which property it is now, but suffice to say that since the Rimes family left over a century ago, there have been no further noises there in the night.

Why is this? It would seem that the visitation was the work of a poltergeist, a word derived from the German for 'noisy spirit'. These noisy and destructive entities haunt people, not property, and in most recorded cases seem to be connected with disturbed teenagers. So, dear reader, if you have a teenager in your home be afraid, be very afraid …

noises duly started in the corridor, causing Wilson to leap out of bed and rush into the hall with the cry of: 'Hallo, here at last are you?' When he reached the corridor, all was silent. As he turned away from the stairs he

5

Ghosts of the City Centre

WHILST Peterborough may have the tag of a 1970s' 'new town', our city centre streets are much older. In 1150, Abbot Martin de Bec launched a plan to create a market and township to finance the building of the new abbey church. The layout that he created as part of this development in Peterborough (as the town was by now called) was essentially the street plan of our modern city centre. Many of the buildings are different, but the streets have changed little in 850 years. With this long history, it is no great surprise that the city's historic heart has many hauntings independent of those in the museum or cathedral precincts.

Priestgate

Priestgate, opposite the Town Hall, is a quiet street. At the far end is Peterborough Museum, which on its own surely contains enough ghosts for any street. However, other buildings here also have stories to tell.

A few doors down from the museum is Yorkshire House, currently home to the Ask Italian restaurant. The building dates to around 1550, when Symon Hake of Thorney – who had recently married and was anxious to show his new status – had it built for himself and his bride. The Hake family lived in the property for the next 300 years, passing it down from one generation to the next; several Hakes served as MPs for the city. A sundial dating to 1660, which survives in the backyard of the property, commemorates the Restoration of the monarchy and the loss of a family member in battle for the Royalist cause during the English Civil War. In the 1840s the property became solicitors' offices (remaining so over the next century), later acting as home to the city's engineer and serving as offices for the Yorkshire Insurance Co. (hence the building's name).

Before the building became a restaurant in 2002, it was occupied by a firm of solicitors called Greenwoods, who then moved to their current offices on Midgate. I have interviewed a number of staff from Greenwoods who worked in Yorkshire House. Many told me that there was something 'odd' about the building, and that strange things happened on the first floor. When working late they would often hear doors banging, and footsteps in the next room or out on the stairs, even if they knew

Yorkshire House, today the Ask restaurant.

only two nights, complaining of footsteps in the dark, doors with a mind of their own, and a dark, hooded figure appearing in the room they were staying in, which leant over them as they lay in their camp beds. Hardly the thing to wake up to! After their experiences, it is no surprise that the men retired to a bed and breakfast instead. Staff who work at Ask tell me that even today this hooded figure, or sometimes a white female one, have been seen upstairs. The good news for diners is that the restaurant is on the ground floor, well away from the ghosts. The bad news is that the toilets are upstairs …

they were the only person there. Some of the solicitors also reported strange occurrences. One said that when he was working late, he would repeatedly get the strong impression that someone – or something – had walked out of the wall opposite his desk, gone across the room and vanished behind him. He said that he sensed rather than saw this entity. The former building manager told me that when locking up at the end of the day, he would walk down the upper corridor and try all the doors to make sure they were locked properly; as he walked on, he would sometimes hear a door rattle behind him, as if someone he couldn't see was also trying the doors.

It is unclear whether Greenwoods mentioned the phenomena when they sold the building to Ask. The first thing that Ask did was bring in builders to convert the place from offices into a restaurant. They used a specialist firm from outside the area, skilled in restaurant installations in historic buildings. Unfortunately, the workmen had to commute some distance to get on-site each day, and these delays meant that the work fell behind schedule. In an attempt to remedy this, they were asked if they wouldn't mind staying on-site – they lasted

Another haunted hostelry in Priestgate is a bar called XXI, which the majority of locals know as the City Club. For most of its history this building was a private members' club for gentlemen, founded in 1882 as the City & Counties Club. Early members included Lord Burghley, and parts of the building (including the members' squash club) still belong to the Burghley estate. The membership remained male-only until the 1980s, and it is only in the last few years that the doors have been opened to non-members.

Bar XXI (formerly the City & Counties Club).

Narrow Bridge Street, c. 1890.

The building has played host to a wide variety of paranormal phenomena, and has been investigated by a number of ghost-hunting groups in recent years. They have reported seeing shadowy figures, and hearing footsteps and voices. On the top floor is a staff flat, next to which is an inaccessible area. This sealed room is only known to be there because there is a chunk of the top floor missing – a window that can be seen from the outside does not correspond with anywhere inside. Why this area is blocked off is unknown, but staff claim to have heard footsteps from inside it. Bar staff have also reported seeing objects move in the bar. A former barman told me that, on a quiet evening, he saw a half-empty pint glass pick itself up from a vacant table and levitate over to another. Keeping an eye on your drink in this establishment would seem to be advisable!

Bridge Street

Bridge Street, stretching from Cathedral Square to the crossing at Bourges Boulevard, was for most of its history known as Narrow Bridge Street, a medieval passage only 22ft wide. The eastern side was demolished and the street widened to admit traffic and make way for the Town Hall. Broad Bridge Street (today Rivergate) continued down to the town bridge and river. In medieval times the street was called Hythegate, as it led down to the hythes (wharves) at the riverside; the word 'gate' derives from the Anglo-Danish word for street, *gaeta*.

Many of the businesses and buildings along Bridge Street report ghostly activity (such as the former Angel Hotel, today WHSmith – *see* Chapter Three). Two other locations here are said to be haunted by employees who are so dedicated that they

Bridge Street, c. 1960. The Town Hall is on the right.

continue to come into work, even from beyond the grave!

The Town Hall dominates Bridge Street, with its grand portico and fine continental-style marble entrance hall, built in 1929. As well as acting as the civic centre, with the Mayor's parlour and council chamber, it houses many council offices and the local primary care trust. Those working in the Town Hall late at night claim to have heard a slow, heavy set of footsteps – but upon investigation have found nobody there. It is thought that this is the ghost of a former security guard who still patrols the building, his distinctive tread recognised by those who knew him in life.

Across the road and on the western side of the street is a distinctive art deco building. Within the premises is Linens Direct, which sells bedding and curtains. The building was erected in 1934 as the Peterborough branch of Burton menswear;

similar buildings were erected in many towns as an early form of architectural branding for the company. Burton continued to have their branch here until they moved into Queensgate in the 1980s.

Former employees of Burton have told me a story about the building – that in the 1960s there was a popular and successful manager who ran the shop. If he had one foible it was excessive tidiness; everything had a place and had to be kept in it. Whenever any new deliveries of stock came in, all the items had to be put away before the doors could be opened for the day. Sadly, the gentleman died of a heart attack long before his time – but this doesn't seem to have been a barrier to him continuing to work.

His replacement as manager was very competent, but less worried about tidiness. When deliveries came in he was more concerned about opening the store than putting things away. Then staff started to realise that things were mysteriously being tidied without them knowing, almost as if an unseen person was cleaning up after them. They came to believe that the spirit of their former boss was, as in life, trying to keep the place tidy. Staff working in the current shop have told me that things still get strangely moved about or tidied.

Cowgate

In medieval times, cattle were driven down Cowgate to the market on the main square, hence the name. Most of the buildings along Cowgate date to the eighteenth or nineteenth century, and are home to speciality shops, restaurants, the city post office and a number of estate agents. Some are haunted.

At the Cathedral Square end of Cowgate, on the corner of Cross Street, a Victorian building accommodates the Peterborough branch of the Prezzo Italian restaurant chain. For most of its history, this site has been a pub. Indeed, it is one of the oldest pub sites in Peterborough, with a medieval tavern here in 1483 called the Falcon, owned by the abbey. In 1897 the premises were rebuilt by William Nichols, who was Mayor of Peterborough for three terms. The building was changed from a pub into the current restaurant in 2004. It is said to have at least two ghosts. The outside corner of the building, facing out onto the corner of the junction of Cross Street and Cowgate, is shaped like a rounded turret. At the first-floor window of the turret, a grey-haired lady in a black Victorian dress has been seen, peering down on the street below in a very disapproving fashion. When the building was a pub, a man was sometimes seen inside propping up the bar,

drinking a pint of beer. Nothing unusual about that – except that the man in question was dressed in Georgian clothing and when approached would vanish.

Further up the street on the right is No. 4 Cowgate, until recently occupied by Fitzjohn Ingle Estate Agents. Staff who worked inside this building claimed to be disturbed in the late afternoon by the eerie sounds of ghostly children laughing and playing in the empty offices upstairs. When anyone plucked up the courage to investigate, nothing strange could be found. Research showed that this part of

Prezzo Italian restaurant, on the corner of Cross Street and Cowgate. A ghostly woman in a black dress has been seen looking out of the first-floor corner window.

The former estate agents on Cowgate. Phantom children have been reported upstairs.

The story relates that some 200 years ago, a stable lad, perhaps seventeen years old, lived and worked in the stables which are now the St John Ambulance building. One day, he went out to the market on the main square to buy some supplies. Browsing at a stall, he looked up and his eyes met those of a pretty young lady of his own age; it was love at first sight. Over the days and weeks that followed, the young couple met regularly. There was just one major problem with their relationship: whilst the young man was a humble stable lad, the young lady was the daughter of a local doctor. Her respectable family would never tolerate her seeing anyone so lowly, so the couple had to meet in secret. This continued until they came to the conclusion that the only way they could be together was for them to elope, and leave Peterborough for a new life elsewhere. They arranged for the wedding to take place and packed their bags in readiness. The appointed afternoon came round, and the young man arrived at the church … but the young lady did not. Whether she'd had second thoughts, or her family found out and stopped her, the story does not relate. The jilted groom was heartbroken

the building was used as a nursery in the early 1900s.

Down the street on the left-hand side is a covered alleyway leading to the St John Ambulance headquarters behind No. 40 Cowgate. The former building dates to the 1700s, and was used as a stable block from 1836 for the parish priest of St John's Church, who lived in the house on Priestgate that backs onto the yard. St John Ambulance has owned the building since 1939; members of this group have reported all sorts of paranormal activity, which may be explained by a legend concerning the building.

The St John Ambulance building. A young man's ghost disappears into the building.

Long Causeway, c. 1900. The left side of the street is now occupied by Queensgate.

and went back to the stables. Feeling that life was not worth living without her, he rummaged around in the yard, found a length of rope, threw it over a beam in the stables and hanged himself.

There is no historical evidence to substantiate the story, but the ghost of a young man has been seen trudging despondently across the yard outside the building, dragging a length of rope, only to disappear into a doorway. He has been seen inside too, making his presence felt on many occasions. A few years ago, the St John Ambulance volunteers had a team photograph taken inside the building, with everyone lined up in their best uniforms. When they looked at the photograph, there was a blurry figure standing alongside that they hadn't seen when the picture was taken. In addition, noises and footsteps were heard around the building as it was being refurbished. A senior St John official was something of a sceptic, and got so fed up with the group talking about the ghost that any mention of it was banned – until the senior official saw it too. The author has spent the night in the building with a group of ghost-hunters, and heard doors banging in response to questions with no apparent explanation; this building definitely has secrets to reveal.

Queensgate

One of the great myths about ghosts is that they only haunt old buildings, but as many of the accounts in this book show, this isn't the case. Sometimes relatively new buildings are haunted because the ghosts themselves are modern – people who simply didn't

1980s' promotional postcard for Queensgate.

night, as they have heard ghostly footsteps and voices, and seen shadowy figures lurking round the building. Some figures have been seen in locked-off areas where there should be no way in or out. In the last few years (at the time of writing) a ghost of a little girl in dirty ragged clothing has been seen, usually around 2 a.m., squatting on the floor and sobbing in the lower mall near to British Home Stores. If approached, she just disappears.

People working in the shops have also had supernatural experiences. Staff at John Lewis claim to have seen a Grey Lady walking through their back room areas, even through the middle of the staff canteen. Workers at a nearby cosmetics store told me that, at the end of the day, they have heard the sound of a little boy laughing at them, almost as if he is playing a game of hide-and-seek. On one occasion they caught a glimpse of him disappearing down a corridor and went to investigate; the corridor was empty. An optician's in the centre is said to be visited by the ghost of a tall elderly gentleman and his Scottish terrier dog, who walk through the shop and disappear into the stockroom at the back; when staff go to check they find nobody there. Other shops have had items mysteriously moved around overnight.

Next time you are in Queensgate, spare a thought; is that person walking past you really there?

Westgate

Another of Peterborough's original streets is Westgate, dominated by Queensgate on one side and by two haunted buildings on the other. One is the Bull Hotel, built in the mid-1700s and described as a coaching inn. The archway through to what would

die that long ago. More often it is because the spirits haunt modern buildings built on very old sites – and the psychic remnants of what used to be there simply haunt the new building that replaced the old. Such is the case with Queensgate.

Many people's main reason for visiting Peterborough is Queensgate, the city's large shopping centre – which is, after the cathedral, the building that dominates the city centre. Opened in March 1982, the centre houses some ninety shops and is a regional shopping destination. In order to build it, streets, shops and houses were demolished in the late 1970s, including the old post office, the Queen Street works occupied by Perkins Engines, and part of the old Cowgate burial ground. Whilst the building may be modern, the site has been inhabited as part of the medieval town for the last 850 years; the ghostly echoes of those who have been there remain, even today.

At night the centre is locked up and empty, apart from security guards who patrol the shops that we see during the day, and the corridors or loading bays that we do not. I have been told that there are areas they feel uncomfortable going into late at

Westgate, c. 1920. The Bull Hotel is on the right.

Peterborough Co-operative, c. 1910; today it is Beales.

have been the stableyard at the back is now the entrance to the hotel. Like many inns the Bull had a 'town pound', meaning that a certain amount of livestock was sometimes accommodated in the outhouses, as a service to the local farmers staying overnight prior to market day. Stables were provided for resident guests in what is now the hotel car park; when the car replaced the horse in the early 1900s, petrol was dispensed from hand pumps at the rear of the hotel.

The Bull may have been built on the site of an early Nonconformist chapel with its own burial ground. In 1999, an extension was built at the rear of the building – and archaeologists had to excavate brick burial vaults and human remains before the foundations could be put in.

These remains may explain some of the ghostly visitations inside the Bull. In the main bar, on a quiet evening, patrons sometimes feel the room go cold and someone brush past them who they cannot see. They also hear a mysterious jingling sound, as if this entity is carrying a large, old-fashioned bunch of keys. Another story, told to me by a member of staff, concerns one of the rooms at the back of the building which is built across the old coachyard. A great lady travelled through the area in the early 1800s by horse-drawn coach, and decided to spend the night at the Bull. The coach was taken to the yard for the lady's luggage to be unloaded, along with her pet dog, which was now let out for the first time after several hours of being cooped up inside. The dog's reaction after this confinement was to relieve itself up the back wheel of the coach, just as the brake was released for the coach to move off. It rolled back, hit the dog and killed it. There is now a hotel room over that site, and staff claim that if they go in to change the sheets, even if the room has been left vacant, they will occasionally find muddy dog paw prints on the bedding.

The other haunted building is what most people locally know as the Westgate Department Store, now called Beales. This is a Victorian building that has a much older ghost. Two ladies who work in the shop have told me that the stockrooms underneath are haunted by a phantom Cavalier, a gentleman in seventeenth-century clothing complete with broad-brimmed hat, long hair and a beard. This particular spirit seems to be aware of those who work in the shop and has a bit of an eye for the ladies; apparently he is in the habit of pinching bottoms!

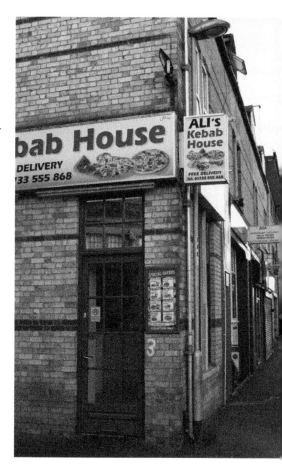

Fitzwilliam Street.

Fitzwilliam Street

Fitzwilliam Street is just off Broadway, tucked between the modern Central Library building and the original Victorian library (now a Chinese restaurant and nightclub). There is a brick nineteenth-century terrace on the left-hand side of the street, which houses several takeaways. A decade ago one of these buildings was a pub, the Flower and Firkin, which developed such a reputation for being haunted that it made its way into the local paper. The building had been a private house, a shop unit and a restaurant before being turned into a pub.

The *Peterborough Evening Telegraph* of 23 October 1998 published an article on the hauntings. Landlady Lorraine Morley described how she always had candles lit in the bar and would snuff them out before leaving. She left the building one night, only to see as she was locking the door that a candle had apparently re-lit itself. She said in the article: 'I thought I might have left a few candles burning, so I went back inside. It was pitch black and the atmosphere sent a tingle up my spine.' Odd sounds and footsteps were heard and a mysterious cold spot was reported on the stairs. The author has spoken to a former barmaid from this pub, who described the ordeal of having to change barrels of beer in the cellar. Unless someone stayed at the top of the cellar steps, the door had a habit of slamming shut, locking the member of staff in the cellar; then the lights would go out. Today the building is a restaurant; the current owners will not say whether such hauntings continue.

6

Greater Peterborough Ghosts

IT is not just the city centre that is haunted; every district, suburb and village in the greater Peterborough area seems to have its own story to tell. Whichever part of the city you live in, work in, or are staying in, there are ghosts. What follows is just a sample of these tales …

The Old Lady at Meynell Walk

One of the suburbs to the west of the city centre is Netherton, composed of houses built in the 1970s by the Peterborough Development Corporation. One of these properties, on Meynell Walk, is owned by a local housing association that has a great deal of difficulty getting a tenant to stay for any length of time. Neighbours say that the house remains empty.

The reason for this is reputed to be the ghost of an elderly lady who haunts the house, believed to be a former tenant who died in the property. The ghost has been seen in the conservatory and goes to visit any resident children when they are in bed at night. That might sound sweet, but imagine you are eight years old, tucked up in bed, fast asleep. Then, you wake to

Meynell Walk in Netherton, where a house is haunted by a former tenant.

hear the bedroom door open; footsteps come into the room; they walk up to the bottom of the bed and you feel someone sit on the bottom. If you can pluck up the courage to pull the duvet back and look, there is nobody there, just a depression in the covers as if someone you can't see is sat there … A former tenant told me that he made multiple attempts to exorcise the house using priests or mediums, but the old lady seems to have no desire to relinquish her tenancy.

The 'Woman in Black' at Woodston

Woodston, south of the river from the city centre, was in such a grip of fear from a terrifying apparition in 1908 that the authorities put up notices warning people about the ghost. The story stayed in people's memories and is still talked of in the area today. In October 1973, the *Peterborough Citizen & Advertiser* featured an article trying to uncover the truth behind the story, interviewing an elderly resident who knew those involved.

The story concerned a lady who lived on Belsize Avenue in 1908, which at that time was inhabited by some of the poorest families in Woodston; it was nicknamed 'the Klondike' by many, as it was reckoned to be so rough. Sadly, the lady died that year. On her deathbed, she was so terrified that her children would be neglected, that she swore she would come back from beyond the grave to watch over them. She was buried in the graveyard at Woodston parish church, but it was said that she kept her deathbed vow.

The witness interviewed by the *Citizen*, Ada Lilly, recalled 'the children, poor little mites that they were, often used to say that their mother was with them when they crossed the road and went out alone'. At the same time, the terrifying spectre of a woman dressed in black began to be seen in the parish churchyard and the public footpath which runs alongside. Many villagers believed that the apparition was the ghost of this lady. The first woman to see the ghost on the path fainted with shock, other sightings becoming common over the weeks that followed. People came from all around to find the ghost. One group of young men equipped themselves with stakes (perhaps confused with vampires) and went to 'lay her ghost once and for all'. What happened to them exactly is unknown, but the six young men appeared at a local pub a few hours later, minus their stakes and absolutely terrified. None of them would ever talk about what happened to them. The reports became so intense that the council put up notices warning people to 'Beware the ghost of the Lady in Black'. At this point, the family of the lady from Belsize Avenue sold up and moved away from the area, and the ghost was never seen again.

The footpath alongside Woodston Church, where the terrifying 'Woman in Black' had its reign of terror in 1908.

The Cherry Tree Pub

Many people claim that their local pub is haunted. Pubs are often old buildings and have had fights, arguments and even murders take place within their walls, adding credence to such stories. It has to be said, however, that many sightings can be put down to an over-indulgence of spirits of a more alcoholic kind.

One of Peterborough's haunted hostelries is also one of our best-known pubs, the Cherry Tree on Oundle Road in Fletton. The pub is known for hosting live music and, being only a short walk from the Peterborough United football ground on London Road, is a great favourite with 'posh' fans on home match days. The building dates back to well before the early 1800s, when the pub was created from two cottages knocked together. Patrons and staff have reported ghostly activity in the pub, claiming that objects have been moved around with nobody there to move them, and items have even been pushed off a shelf. The apparition of a gentleman dressed in Victorian clothing and smoking a clay pipe has also been seen in one of the public bars.

The Cherry Tree pub on Oundle Road.

The Bretton Park Couple

Bretton was one of the first suburbs to be created by the Peterborough Development Corporation in the early 1970s. As a relatively modern area, built across former farmland, it would seem strange to find ghost stories here. However, to the north, beyond the Cresset centre, supermarket and retail park, is a grassed parkland bordered by housing estates. Local people walking or cycling across this area of an evening might see an elderly couple dressed in dark clothing walking across the park. They look quite normal, and as you walk past them they will perhaps nod and smile at you. But as you walk on, if you happen to glance back you will see them just fade away into thin air.

The Garton End Ghost

Another ghost reported by the *Peterborough Advertiser*, on 16 April 1926, was seen in the lane between Garton End and Dogsthorpe. This short, dark, hooded apparition was witnessed by a number of people.

It was first seen just before the preceding Christmas by a local lady, who was said to have been so terrified by the sighting that she would not leave her house for a month. Charles Johnson of Cherry Tree Cottage in Garton End claimed to be something of a ghost-hunter, and set out to investigate his local ghost. After several attempts he managed to get a sighting of the apparition, and described what happened as follows:

> Last Friday night I was in the lane, proceeding from Dogsthorpe to Garton End. It would be about ten minutes to ten, and suddenly, right in front of me, at about 20 to 30 yards away, appeared a black hooded

Above: *Path through Bretton Park, where the ghosts of an elderly couple have been seen.*

Right: *Artist's impression of the 'Garton End Ghost'.* (Peterborough Advertiser, 16 April 1926)

figure of about five feet in height. The hood came right down to the ground, and the figure seemed to be gliding along two or three feet from the footpath. I at once bolted forward, and as I did so the figure glided rapidly away, and seemed to melt through the hedge …

Johnson searched high and low, but could find no sign of it.

Over the following week, Johnson saw it twice more. Asked if he thought the ghost was genuine, he replied, 'I'm blowed if I know … this is the first time I have seen anything bordering on the unnatural. I confess I cannot understand this.' Two

The old Memorial Hospital, until 2010 part of Peterborough District Hospital.

The visitors' entrance to the Perkins engineering plant at Eastfield.

The Bell Hotel, Stilton; one of the many places nationally said to be haunted by the famed highwayman Dick Turpin.

other witnesses were interviewed and the paper speculated that the ghost was that of a local 'Rag and Bone' lady called Mrs Clements, nicknamed 'One-legged Peggy', who had died in the Workhouse Infirmary two years before. The author has interviewed a local resident who claims to have seen a similar figure in the area within the last decade, so perhaps the Garton End ghost has not ceased to put in appearances!

The Memorial Hospital Ghost

The Memorial Hospital opened on Thorpe Road as a purpose-built replacement for the Infirmary (*see* Chapter One). The author has been told by many medical staff who worked in this building that the spectral figure of a nurse was sometimes seen on a ward in the Memorial Wing. She walked through the ward, disappearing into a bricked-up doorway at the end of the room. The apparition's identity is unknown, but staff believed her to be a warning ghost, appearing when a mistake or overdose was about to occur that could harm a patient. I have spoken to at least three people who claim to have seen her, all under these circumstances.

Industrial Ghosts at Perkins Engines

One of the great engineering names associated with Peterborough is that of Perkins Engines. Perkins was established in a garage unit on Queen Street in 1932 by Frank Perkins, to manufacture diesel car engines. During the Second World War, production was switched to produce boat engines for the Royal Navy, the profits from which funded the Eastfield works, the home of Perkins since 1947. At one time, around a quarter of the working population in the city were employed by Perkins; it is still one of our biggest employers and the company is known worldwide for producing quality diesel engines for heavy plant vehicles, tractors and boats.

I have done ghost walks for groups of Perkins employees, many of whom have told me stories of phantoms which haunt the Eastfield works. The story I have been told most commonly goes back to the late 1980s, and concerns a university student from outside of Peterborough who was working for an agency as temporary security guard. He was drafted in one night to work a shift at the Perkins site, and arrived at 6 p.m. to be briefed and shown around. Equipped with a radio to keep in contact with the control room, he set out on patrol around the site. Around 11 p.m. he was passing the administration block, one of the older buildings on the site, which was locked up and in darkness. As he was passing by, he looked up and was astonished to see a light go on at a top-floor window. He radioed through to the control room to ask for advice; before he got an answer, he saw a man's face appear at the window. He described him as a balding elderly man with a moustache, who waved at him before he turned away from the window.

A few moments later, the young man's supervisor arrived with the keys. The window by now was empty, but the light was still on. The two men unlocked the building and went upstairs to investigate; by the time they got there the light was off and there was no sign of anyone. The supervisor took the rather shaken young man back to the control room, gave him a cup of tea, and asked him to look in a photo album to see if he could pick out the man he'd seen.

After a moment, the young man pointed to a picture.

'There, that's the man I saw!'

The supervisor nodded. 'Thought so. That's Frank Perkins, the founder of the company. He died in 1967, but his office used to be up there. You're not the only person to have seen him …'

The Haunted Hostelry – the Bell Hotel in Stilton

The Bell Inn is probably the best-known building in Stilton, the village just off the A1 a few miles to the south of Peterborough. The Bell has stood on its present site since at least 1500, possibly as far back as 1437. The current building dates from 1642 and is one of the finest examples of a seventeenth-century coaching inn in the country, built to service the needs of travellers on the Great North Road between London and York. It is famed for being the birthplace of Stilton cheese – Daniel Defoe staying there and writing of this 'English Parmesan' in 1724.

Legend has it that the famed highwayman Dick Turpin stayed at the inn, supposedly hiding there for nine weeks while hunted by the law. Surprised by a raid, he threw open the window and jumped onto his horse Black Bess to gallop off up the Great North Road. Dick Turpin's spirit is believed to be one of the ghosts that haunt the Bell.

In 1962 a new landlord moved into the Bell, then after several days asked locals about the atmosphere in one of the bedrooms. He told them that a fire had suddenly ignited in the grate, despite the fact that nobody had lit it. He was told that the bedroom was the one in which Turpin is reputed to have slept. A year later,

the landlord acquired a large dog which began howling soon after midnight on Wednesdays – the night when it is said that Turpin's spirit is most active and wanders the passages of the inn. Guests have reported seeing the apparition of a dark figure on horseback outside, or have been woken early in the morning to see a dark figure standing at the bottom of their bed.

Turpin's ghost is not the only one said to haunt the hotel. Several customers have asked after a woman dressed in period clothes, whom they've passed in the corridor and presumed was a hotel employee. Staff regularly report equipment being moved or disappearing from the bar or kitchen only to reappear several days later, or get the feeling of being watched and seeing shadowy figures in their peripheral vision. One table in the restaurant has the reputation of being cursed; lots of accidents have happened around it, and over the years at least three customers have allegedly died whilst sitting there.

The Grey Lady at Thorpe Hall

Drive into Peterborough city centre from the south, along the Thorpe parkway, and you will see a large area of grassed parkland to your left, dominated by a great mansion. This is Thorpe Hall, built between 1653 and 1656 for Oliver St John, son-in-law and Lord Chief Justice to Oliver Cromwell. The house was one of the few mansions built during the 1650s and is the finest Commonwealth period mansion in the country. In 1654 it was described by the diarist John Evelyn as 'a stately place … built out of the ruins of the Bishop's Palace and Cloisters'. Much of the original panelling survives downstairs, and these rooms and the wonderful landscaped gardens are open regularly throughout the year. The hall served as a maternity hospital from 1943 to 1970, and since 1986 it has been used by the Sue Ryder Foundation as a hospice.

For many years, long before Sue Ryder took over the property, people have claimed that Thorpe Hall and its grounds are haunted. Visitors have seen a gardener in Victorian clothing in the grounds, who will just evaporate into thin air.

The best-known ghost at the hall is that of the Grey Lady, who has been seen on many occasions inside the building, most commonly on the main staircase. One lady, who lives in Longthorpe village, told me about her experience of seeing the Grey Lady in the autumn of 1985. The woman was walking her dog, a large Alsatian, through the grounds of the hall (which at that time was vacant). As she went past, she peered into a couple of windows. She attracted the attention of the caretaker, who, seeing her interest in the property, asked if she would like to have a look around. Accompanied by the dog, he showed the lady around the ground floor, until they reached the main staircase. As they reached the bottom of the steps, they were astonished and horrified to see a grey female figure gliding down the stairs; as it reached the top of the last flight of steps, the figure disappeared into thin air. It was not the only one that did a disappearing act – the dog had taken one look at the figure and fled in the opposite direction, wrenching its lead out of the lady's hand in its panic. It took the lady some time to recover her dog, by which time it had run halfway across the park outside.

The Haunted Cottage at Upton

To the west of Peterborough are several villages around Castor. These communities have some of the longest histories in the area, with evidence found of Roman and Anglo-Saxon occupation. There are a number of ghost stories around here, but

Thorpe Hall, where the figure of a Grey Lady has been seen.

the best-documented concerns a thatched cottage in Upton. The story was covered in detail in a series of newspaper accounts in the *Peterborough Advertiser* in March 1920, which are interesting as they show how much a ghost story can be exaggerated.

An article published on 13 March sets out the story. The house concerned was the end property of a row of four thatched cottages owned by the Fitzwilliam estate. Some five weeks previously, a new family had moved into the house: Mr John Macro, his wife and two young daughters. Mr Macro had gained a position as a tree-feller for the Fitzwilliams. Shortly after taking up residence, the family started to hear strange sounds – an unexplained clapping sound in the pantry and in one of the bedrooms. Mr Macro was interviewed, and explained what happened next:

> We had heard some funny noises ever since we first came to Upton. One night I went upstairs for something after dark and did not take a light with me. When I got inside the bedroom, I was amazed to see a tall, thin woman in white standing there. Her head seemed to be swathed and I could not see her face, but only her figure. As I looked it moved slowly about half-way round the room and then disappeared into thin air! It was just like vapour …

Mr Macro saw the ghost on a couple of occasions thereafter but said nothing to his family, until one of his daughters woke up to find the woman in white leaning over her. Then, two nights in succession, a strange creature – 15in in length, with a tail and making a noise 'like the starting of a motor car' – appeared downstairs through a window and disappeared in the bedroom with no trace; at the same time, the White Lady would again appear. Eventually the

family started to sleep with the lights on, which seemed to be the only thing that discouraged the strange events from taking place. The newspaper speculated that previous residents had fled the house, that an old lady had died there and that the local rector had stayed overnight to try to see the ghost.

A week later, the 20 March edition of the *Advertiser* had to retract some parts of the story. Interviews with Mr Fitzwilliam and the previous occupant of the house, and a testy letter from the rector, clarified that nobody had fled the house previously, that there had been no known ghost sightings before, and no ghost-hunt. The rector believed that the black creature was merely some form of bird or insect and advised any ghost-hunters to desist, warning off any more 'long-haired cranks who may waste their time'. However, no explanation was offered for the White Lady and the Macros stuck resolutely to their story in this regard. Whether sightings have been reported by later occupants is unknown.

The White Lady of Orton Hall

In one of Peterborough's southern suburbs is Orton Longueville Hall, today a luxury hotel. Most of this mansion dates to the 1700s, although parts are older and, during recent building works, Anglo-Saxon burials were found on-site. From 1791 the hall was the home of the Huntly family. Charles, the 10th Marquess, his second wife Marie Antonietta, and their family of fourteen children (two of whom died in infancy) made their home at Orton for most of the nineteenth century. The couple were fascinated by natural history and travelled around Europe collecting specimens of plants and flowers, some of which they planted in the parkland at Orton, including

Orton Hall. Staff claim to have seen a phantom White Lady in the building.

its famed specimens of Wellingtonia trees. Charles died in 1863, Marie Antoinetta in 1893; the Huntly family retained the property until 1937. During the Second World War, the mansion was used as a prisoner-of-war camp, then post-war as a special school. In recent years it has become the luxury hotel that it is today.

A number of ghost stories have circulated about the property, including sightings of a prisoner-of-war, but the best known and most persistent ghost is that of a White Lady. The author has spoken to many staff and even managers at the hotel who claim to have experienced this particular haunting. The White Lady is said to pick on male members of staff; some are quite nervous about going into certain parts of the building, at least on their own. One told me that he had been 'propelled' down a corridor by an unseen force.

Another staff member told me that a female manager was asked if she would stay as duty manager overnight whilst there was a large function at the hotel. She agreed on condition that she could have a good suite to stay in with her husband, as it happened to be their wedding anniversary that night. Apparently neither of the couple got a decent night's sleep, both claiming that they were being touched, poked or prodded by icy hands ... despite the fact that they were not touching each other!

On another occasion, staff tried an experiment to see if they could catch the ghost on film. They set up a video camera in a conference room in which the ghost had been seen, and locked the door. All the keys were taken offsite by a manager who was going home for the night – so there could be no accusations of interference, as nobody could get into the room. The following morning, they unlocked the door and were astonished to find the video camera had been knocked off its stand and was on the floor. When they played back the footage, they saw the curtains apparently opening and closing by themselves ...

Ferry Meadows Hauntings

Ferry Meadows Country Park, managed by Nene Park Trust, is 500 acres of parkland, lakes and woodland just to the south of the River Nene. The site has a visitor centre, watersports lake, nature trails and miniature railway; it is probably the most visited attraction in the city and one of Peterborough's green spaces.

The area has a long history, prehistoric remains and Roman buildings having been excavated on-site. Most of the excavation work took place in the 1970s, to provide materials for roads around Peterborough as part of the new town development. The quarries were then flooded to create the lakes that we see today. Nene Park Trust was created in 1988 to manage the site.

At Ferry Meadows and its sister site at Orton Mere, a number of witnesses claim to have seen a phantom lorry. The story is that this lorry was involved in an accident on the site, careering off a cliff into a quarry and killing the driver. I can find no record of any such accident taking place to substantiate this story.

Another ghost has been seen near the Milton Ferry Bridge, which crosses the Nene at the north side of Ferry Meadows. The bridge dates to 1716, when it was built by the Hon. William Fitzwilliam and used until the 1960s as a toll bridge, charging pedestrians and light traffic heading to and from Alwalton. On the south bank of the river, a phantom highwayman has been seen on horseback, often in broad daylight. He gallops across the ground near the bridge and disappears into a stand of trees nearby. One witness to this particular haunting is a park ranger, who told me that he saw the highwayman in 2010. He searched the woods where the figure had disappeared but could find no sign of it. In November 2011, a colleague within the Vivacity trust asked me about the highwayman; her parents had reported seeing it just a few days beforehand.

Orton Mere. A phantom lorry has been reported here and at nearby Ferry Meadows.

'Button Cap' and the Rectory at Barnack

South-west of Barnack parish church, a few miles to the north of Peterborough city centre, is the local rectory. The earliest parts of the building are medieval, with the main house added in 1880. The local rector in the 1820s was Charles Kingsley, whose son, also called Charles, became a social campaigner and novelist, best known as the author of *The Water Babies*. As a child at the rectory, Charles and his siblings were taught Latin, mathematics, botany, natural history and drawing by their father. Charles composed

Kingsley House, the former rectory at Barnack.

poems from the age of four, some of which show a preoccupation with death.

Barnack Rectory was reputed to be haunted by a ghost called 'Button Cap' in a bedroom in the north wing. This ghost was supposedly a former rector who wore a flowered dressing gown and a cap with a button on it, hence the name. In life the man was said to have defrauded a widow and orphan, so his restless ghost was thought to be searching for evidence of the incriminating deed. Charles, as a young child, was moved to the haunted room when suffering from brain fever and became a victim of dreams and nightmares. Some of these were adapted and included in his novels. Young Charles claimed to have seen the ghost, although as an adult he denied this and dismissed the story.

The Vengeful Spectre at Elton Hall

Elton Hall is a stately home on the western edge of the old Soke of Peterborough, set within parkland bounded by the River Nene to the north. The house and gardens are open to the public at certain times during the summer months.

Since the Norman Conquest there has been a house on this site, held for much of its history by the Sapcote family. Parts of the present house were built by Sir Richard Sapcote in the mid-1400s. In 1617, the Sapcotes sold the estate to Sir Nathaniel Riche. It is unclear what happened next, but by 1664 Sir Thomas Proby owned the house. He pulled down much of the medieval hall in 1665, leaving only the gateway

Elton Hall, from the gardens.

and chapel, and rebuilt the house to suit his own needs – work that was completed by his brother, John Proby. In 1750, John Proby (created Lord Carysfort in 1752) married an Irish heiress and acquired large estates in Ireland. The house and estate continued to grow over the years, and the hall is currently home to Sir William Proby and his family.

Legend has it that a ghostly figure appears by a small clump of trees close to the hall. This spectre is said to be that of Robert Sapcote, who died in 1600, the last member of that family to live at Elton. He was an inveterate gambler who did not like losing at cards, and arranged for servants or hired thugs to rob his guests on their way home if he had lost too much money to them. Several of his regular guests got so fed up with this treatment that they arranged for some men to lie in wait in the garden, and give Sapcote a taste of his own medicine with a heavy beating.

Unfortunately, it seems to have gone too far and Sapcote died of his injuries. His vengeful ghost, a dark figure in a black cloak with a large black dog, is said to stalk the grounds. This story has been handed down through the generations in Elton, with parents telling their children, 'You will have old Sapcote after you!' if they go into certain parts of the park after dark.

Thorney's Ghostly Tales

To the eastern edge of greater Peterborough is the village of Thorney. For much of its history, Thorney was an island rising above the surrounding fens. Archaeological work in the village in recent years has shown that there was a settlement there from the Bronze Age to the Romans, ancient people cultivating the rich farmland. In 662 a Christian community of monks was established on this island, then known as

Ancarig, or the Island of the Hermits. This community was attacked by the Vikings in 870, although it is said that the monks escaped the attack and then helped to bury the monks of Peterborough who were not so fortunate.

The settlement was re-established with an abbey on the island, one of the 'fen five' monastic houses which survived until the Reformation. The fen area was drained in the seventeenth century under the influence of the landowners, the Russell family. Much of the housing in the core of the village was built by the estate; then in 1910 the Russell family sold Thorney. During the twentieth century the village has become a residential area, still dominated by the monastic church which survives as the parish church.

Thorney also has its own hauntings; villagers have told me that they have seen shadowy figures in the local community centre at Bedford Hall – according to one lady, they are Civil War soldiers. Others have simply heard footsteps or heard doors banging by themselves.

On the edge of the village is a large pond, known to most local people as 'the pit'. Folklore has it that this is sometimes the scene of a ghostly re-enactment, depicting a tragic accident which occurred some 200 years ago when a coach and horses crashed off the road into the pond, killing all the occupants.

Another curious story involves one of the old estate cottages at the heart of the village, bought a few years ago by a gentleman who was renovating it with the help of his

The Bedford Hall at Thorney, housing the Thorney Museum and the Community Hall.

father. Whilst working in the house they were listening to Radio 2, but after a few days they started to hear the channel changing on the radio, apparently all by itself. The younger man walked into the kitchen when this happened one day, and was astonished to see the dial on the radio turning – as if someone he couldn't see was retuning it! It seemed that he had a ghostly housemate that was making its presence felt.

Early 1700s' engraving of Burghley House.

Is Burghley House Haunted?

Whilst the gates of the Burghley estate lead directly into the lovely town of Stamford in Lincolnshire, the house and most of the estate are (and always have been) in Peterborough. The walls edging the magnificent parkland, which is famed for its annual horse trials, mark the boundary of the old Soke and modern authority area of the city of Peterborough.

Burghley is famed as being one of the finest stately homes in the country, and is certainly the grandest surviving mansion of the Elizabethan age. It was built between 1555 and 1587 by William Cecil, Lord Burghley, Chief Minister to Queen Elizabeth I and the greatest statesman of his age. The house is furnished lavishly, thanks to the 5th Earl of Exeter's travels around the Continent and his purchase of many works of art; the house has a fine collection of Canaletto paintings (not on display in the public rooms), amongst many other treasures. As well as being a popular destination for visitors, the house has been made famous as a filming location, featuring in the recent film adaptation of *Pride and Prejudice*.

I am often asked if Burghley is haunted. Publicly, the existence of ghosts in the house is sidestepped by the estate. The closest we have to an admission of something paranormal in the house is in Lady Victoria Leatham's book, *Burghley: The Life of a Great House*, where she says of the 4th George stateroom: 'If we were to acknowledge a ghost at Burghley, this is the room in which he would belong.' She goes on to say that a member of staff, when locking up this room, heard a man's voice say: 'Oh, a pox on it.' On another occasion, a tall male figure in black was seen standing by the fireplace in this room.

Tour guides at Burghley have told me that they have had reports from visitors of odd phenomena in the house; some visitors have had similar experiences to those mentioned concerning the 4th George room; many people say they feel inexplicably uncomfortable in the Queen Elizabeth bedroom; whilst others have said they feel strangely cold in the 3rd George room, despite it being south-facing and one of the warmest rooms in the house. It would be strange if a magnificent and historic property like Burghley didn't have at least one ghost!

Afterword

What is a Ghost?

THEORIES about what ghosts are, and if they exist in the first place, abound within the scientific community, the media, and some of the more esoteric interest groups. The view amongst most 'believers' is that there are several types of so-called ghosts.

Many appear as images, noises or even smells, with no active 'intelligence', and are simply replays of a particular historical event or moment. Often these 'tape-recordings' of the past are of mundane events, which were perhaps repeated on a day-to-day basis; more rarely, they show a particular moment of high emotion, such as a violent death. This explanation, known as the 'stone tape theory', suggests that electrical energy of some kind has seeped into the very fabric of a place and can be replayed when the right conditions (such as the environment or time) are met. This image appears the same, irrespective of any building changes, which explains why many ghost sightings are of figures walking through walls or floors – any changes to the building since the 'recording' was made are irrelevant to the haunting, and the ghost continues to follow the route it took in life. Other hauntings can be more random and activity seems to be guided or intelligent. This is thought to be 'spirit' activity, involving the spirit or soul of an individual (rather than just their image).

How or when to see a ghost? In my experience, when you least expect to. From the testimonies of people I've interviewed, you're just as likely to see a ghost during the day as late at night, and it can affect people from all walks of life and backgrounds – even sceptics! I find it fascinating that many people who tell me about their ghostly experiences prefix their stories with: 'I never used to believe in ghosts until …'

There has been an explosion of interest in the paranormal in Britain in recent years, partly as a result of the number of books, ghost walks and television programmes (notably Living TV's *Most Haunted*) on the subject. I suspect that part of the interest also stems from a kind of post-millennial need for belief and answers to the big questions – such as whether there is life after death, or what the meaning of life is – particularly with the decline in organised religion. We are all a sucker for a good ghost story and a scare, even if we claim not to believe in ghosts!

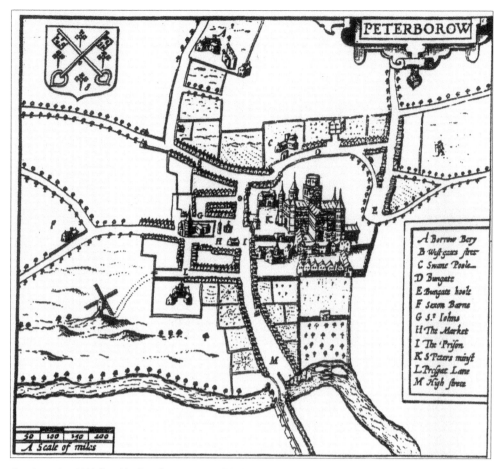

Peterborough in 1611, from John Speed's county map of Northamptonshire.

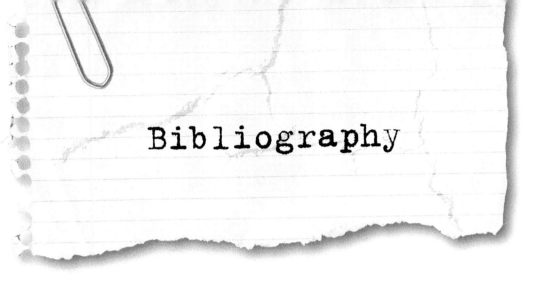

Bibliography

Books

Barcroft, M., *Luckiest of All* (Minimax, 1983)

Bendixson, T., *The Peterborough Effect: Reshaping a City* (Peterborough Development Corporation, 1988)

Bevis, T., *Cambridgeshire Fens: Landscapes and Legends* (Cottage Publications, 2010)

Boulton, D., *A Square Deal All Round: The History of Perkins Engines* (Perkins Engines, 2007)

Brandon, D. & Knight, J., *Peterborough Past: The City and The Soke* (Phillimore, 2001)

Brooks, J.A., *Railway Ghosts* (Jarrold, 1989)

Chamberlain, P., *Hell Upon Water: Prisoners of War in Britain, 1793–1815* (The History Press, 2008)

Codd, D., *Mysterious Cambridgeshire* (Derby Books Publishing, 2010)

Davies, C., *Stamford and the Civil War* (Paul Watkins, 1992)

Dixon, G., *Folk Tales and Legends of Cambridgeshire* (Minimax, 1987)

Forman, J., *Haunted East Anglia* (Fontana, 1974)

Frayling, C., *Nightmare: Birth of Horror* (BBC Books, 1996)

Gray, D., *Peterborough, City at War* (Gray Press, 2011)

Gunton, S., *A History of the Cathedral Church of Peterborough* (Paul Watkins, 1990)

Herbert, W.B., *Railway Ghosts & Phantoms* (David & Charles, 1989)

Hillier, R., *Clay that Burns: A History of the Fletton Brick Industry* (London Brick, 1981)

Howat, P., *Ghosts and Legends of Cambridgeshire* (Countryside Books, 1998)

Jones, R., *Haunted Houses of Britain and Ireland* (New Holland, 2005)

Jones, R., *Haunted Britain* (AA Publishing, 2010)

Leatham, V., *Burghley: The Life of a Great House* (Herbert Press, 1992)

Liquorice, M. (Ed), *Posh Folk: Notable Personalities (and a Donkey) Associated with Peterborough* (Cambridgeshire Libraries, 1991)

Mellows, W.T. (Ed), *The Peterborough Chronicle of Hugh Candidus* (Peterborough Museum Society, 1941)

Metcalfe, L., *Discovering Ghosts* (Shire Publications, 1994)

Orme, S., (Ed.) Various – Articles for *Musings*, Journal of Friends of Peterborough Museum on Ghosts, 2001–8

Orme, S. (Ed), Various – *People of Peterborough, Volume 1* (Peterborough Museum Publishing, 2009)

Orme, S. (Ed), Various – *People of Peterborough, Volume 2* (Peterborough Museum Publishing, 2011)

Porter, E., *Cambridgeshire Customs & Folklore* (Routledge, 1969)

Simmons, G., *Wings over Westwood: The Story of RAF Peterborough* (GMS, 1989)

Smith, M., *Stamford Myths & Legends* (Paul Watkins, 1998)

Tebbs, H.F., *Peterborough: A History* (Oleander Press, 1979)

Upex, S., *The Romans in the East of England* (The History Press, 2008)

Various, *Peterborough: A Story of City and Country, People and Places* (Pitkin Unichrome Ltd, 2000)

Walker, T.J., *The Depot for Prisoners of War at Norman Cross* (BiblioBazaar, 2009)

Whyman, P., *Dead Haunted: Paranormal Encounters and Investigations* (New Holland, 2007)

Newspapers

Peterborough Citizen & Advertiser
Peterborough Evening Telegraph
Peterborough Standard

Index

If you enjoyed this book, you may also be interested in…

Haunted Spalding
GEMMA KING

Featuring hair-raising first-hand accounts of unexplained sightings and paranormal phenomena, this eerie and richly illustrated tour around the historic town of Spalding contains many chilling stories. Amongst the spooky tales are a pub where a resident ghost hurled a beer bottle at a member of staff, a hotel where a mischievous spirit sits on the beds and leaves ghostly handprints on a mirror, and the evil spirit so intent on harassing a local family that it could only be removed by exorcism.

978 0 7524 6992 8

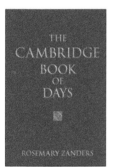

Haunted Bedford
WILLIAM H. KING

From heart-stopping accounts of apparitions and manifestations to eerie encounters with phantoms and spirits, this collection of stories reveals Bedford's darker side. Drawing on historical and contemporary sources, *Haunted Bedford* examines some of the lively characters that are said to haunt the town, including the ghost of famous author John Bunyan and Black Tom the highwayman, who was executed here.

978 0 7524 6592 0

The Cambridge Book of Days
ROSEMARY ZANDERS

Taking you through the year day by day, *The Cambridge Book of Days* contains a quirky, eccentric, amusing or important event or fact from different periods of history, many of which had a major impact on the religious, scientific and political history of England as a whole. Ideal for dipping into, this addictive little book will keep you entertained and informed. Featuring hundreds of snippets of information, it will delight residents and visitors alike.

978 0 7524 5953 0

Folklore of Lincolnshire
SUSANNA O'NEILL

The county of Lincolnshire is a beautiful mixture of low-lying marshy fen land, modest hills and the steep valleys of the rolling Wolds; it is also home to a wealth of folklore, legend and intrigue. This vast region is rich in superstitions, songs and traditional games. A study of the daily life, lore and customs of Lincolnshire are here interspersed with stories of monstrous black hounds, dragon lairs, witches, mischievous imps and tales of the people known as the Yellowbellies.

978 0 7524 5964 6

Visit our website and discover thousands of other History Press books.
www.thehistorypress.co.uk